THE RADICAL LIBERAL
The New Politics:
Theory and Practice

ARNOLD S. KAUFMAN
University of California, Los Angeles

FOREWORD BY Hans J. Morgenthau

A CLARION BOOK
Published by Simon and Schuster

FOR MY FATHER AND MOTHER

A Clarion Book
Published by Simon and Schuster
Rockefeller Center, 630 Fifth Avenue
New York, New York 10020

Copyright © 1968 by Atherton Press
Reprinted by arrangement with Atherton Press
Portions of this book have appeared in Dissent

SECOND PAPERBACK PRINTING

SBN 671-20576-5
Manufactured in the United States of America

CONTENTS

FOREWORD

Hans J. Morgenthau

UNIVERSITY OF CHICAGO

The crisis of American politics is in the main the result of three factors. One is the shift of effective power from the people to the government. The second lies in the nature of the problems to be solved through political action. The third is to be found in the inadequacy of the political concepts which we bring to bear on the problems to be solved.

These three factors are interconnected in that they flow from the technological revolutions that have transformed man's relations to nature and his position within society. These technological changes have enormously increased the powers of the government vis-à-vis the people. The monopolistic possession of the most destructive weapons of warfare and the centralized control of the mass media of communications have made the government virtually immune from what used to be a permanent threat and, hence, a permanent source of restraint: popular revolution.

Compared with the great political issues of fifty or a hundred years ago, the issues we are called upon to deal with today, such as the avoidance of nuclear war or racial integration, are both less intelligible and more intractable. A century ago, it was a simple matter to make up one's mind about the merits of slavery or of the compulsory arbitration of international disputes, and once one had made up one's mind, it was a simple matter to put that decision into practice. Today the complexities of nuclear warfare and of racial equality appear to defy the intellectual grasp of the man in the street and stand in the way of simple, clear-cut solutions.

Finally, we try to comprehend, and act upon, the political world through intellectual categories belonging to an age that has passed. How relevant is the traditional opposition between right and left for the political issues of the day? Can the political philosophies of conservatism, liberalism, fascism, socialism, communism tell us something which will help us to understand and master the contemporary political world? These questions have not been answered. Consequently, political philosophy has tended to become ritualistic incantation, in good measure intellectually irrelevant and politically useless, save as ideological rationalization and justification. Large masses of the citizenry have tended to give up the political game altogether, retreating in frustration into their private spheres and leaving political decisions to the experts who are supposed to know best. On the other hand, the activists of the "New Left" tend to negate meaningful political action by asserting the Rousseauist goodness and freedom of the individual against the fetters of political society of any kind.

Professor Kaufman has set himself the task of supplying answers to these philosophic questions. He does so by trying to rediscover the original meaning of the liberal tenets and apply them to the most urgent political problems of the day. That such a task is intellectually worthwhile is beyond doubt. For the great political philosophies of the past, by dint of having weathered the ravages of time, have proven to contain a core of rational truth which continues to appeal to the rational nature of man. That rational truth is hidden, distorted, and corrupted by the political interests that in a particular period of history have used it for their purposes. Every historic epoch has the task of discovering anew that rational truth by separating it from its ephemeral historic formulations and applications.

But the task Professor Kaufman has set himself does not end here. After rediscovering the liberal tenets, as it were, in their pure form, he tries to show the relevance of these tenets for the understanding and mastery of the contemporary political world. Here the task of the historian and analyst of political ideas merges with that of the activist philosopher of politics. His success or failure in this latter respect depends not only upon his qualifications as a political philosopher but also upon the susceptibility of political reality to his teachings. Professor Kaufman has gone as far as a political philosopher can go: he has rediscovered the rational essence of liberalism and brought it to bear upon the contemporary political scene. How the political scene will react will be decided by history, not by philosophy.

PREFACE

The manuscript of this book was completed almost three years ago. Since then, the new politics has become a potent reality of American life. What started with the teach-in movement grew and eventually became the Dump-Johnson movement, the Kennedy and McCarthy primary campaigns, the New Democratic Coalition with affiliates in over thirty-five states, and, most recently, the Vietnam Moratorium with its astonishing display of issue-focused political energy. Meanwhile, parallel movements within minority communities have grown—for example, successful or nearly successful black candidates for high office in major metropolitan centers and the very effective Grape Boycott by César Chavez's United Farmworkers' Union. These developments suggest that a fundamental transformation of the American political process is taking place.

Though there is much talk about the new politics, there is little precise description of what it is and how it differs from the old politics or from the kind of militancy in which political activity is seen mainly as an opportunity for confrontation and ecstasy.

My view is that the new politics has five essential and distinguishing characteristics. All were intimated in my book, but recent developments have made it possible to be more definite and clear about what they are.

First, those in the new politics are committed to the view that only radical reconstruction of fundamental institutions —political, industrial, educational, and, more broadly, cultural—can fulfill the promise of American life.

Second, despite an ever increasing volume of liberal-baiting (SDS's *New Left Notes*, for example, claimed that the October 15th Vietnam Moratorium was a liberal effort to destroy the peace movement), the rank and file of the new politics believe that radical change is necessary *because* they are authentically liberal. Increasingly they call themselves "radical liberals."

Third, the new politics is based on the conviction that working through established processes of American democracy can foster radical change. The dark pessimism of militants who regard conventional politicking as a form of co-optation is repudiated. There are, however, important disagreements within the new politics. While all retain faith in electoral effort, some favor formation of a new party, others favor working mainly upon and within the Democratic Party.* Though these convictions are strongly, sometimes abrasively held, the resulting conflict is a family quarrel in comparison with all that divides the new politics from the two contrasting forms.

A fourth essential characteristic of the new politics is

---

* I have elsewhere argued that the strategy of working on and in the Democratic Party is preferable to organizing a new party. Cf. "Strategies for New Politics," *Dissent*, January-February, 1969, pp. 12–19.

really a corollary of continued faith in the potentialities of the electoral process. The men and women of the new politics take a dim view of violence and disorder as ways of achieving desirable radical change. But their opposition is mainly tactical, not principled. That is, they are not prepared to pledge non-violence. They are too well aware of the historic rigidities of the democratic process; too well aware of the fact that violence and disorder have been important, even necessary, parts of successful efforts to end slavery, to win the franchise for women, to force recognition of trade unions, and, most recently, to achieve a modest increment of justice for black, brown, and red Americans. Most new politics people are not, therefore, prepared to convert tactical opposition to violence and disorder into absolute principles of political morality. They have evaluated and will continue to evaluate the desirability of such tactics case by case. But they are convinced that, at this moment, departure from peaceful political effort produces little political benefit in the United States.

The fifth distinguishing characteristic of the new politics is the one that sets it off most definitely from the old politics. The new politics is principally a politics of issues, not candidates. Loyalty to party, loyalty to candidates, winning elections are important only as they contribute to the fulfillment of the radical liberal's programs and values. Those who practice the new politics are therefore ready to exercise an electoral veto on Democratic candidates when doing so serves their concern for issues. The new politics implies rejection of the pseudo-realistic politics of "the lesser evil." For a lesser evil in the short run can be the instrument of social and political disaster in the long run. It was the endless succession of lesser-evil candidates that permitted America's gravest social evils to fester until they exploded in open crisis. The new politics implies predominant concern with the overall dynamic of the political process, not the grubby ambitions of lesser-evil politicians.

This new politics of issues was most dramatically revealed in the Vietnam Moratorium, which surprised even its organizers by tapping energies of unsuspected scope and intensity. The Moratorium provided the proof that was needed that the McCarthy and Kennedy campaigns were based on qualities more important than the charisma of two superb Americans. A political event without precedent in American political history, the Moratorium is the natural descendant of all that was best in the teach-in movement, now moved off the campuses into homes, churches, union halls, business establishments, even Wall Street's paladiums of finance. Like the teach-ins, the Moratorium was organized without visible national leadership—and certainly without reliance on any particular candidate. As with the teach-ins, those who had habitually followed led, and political leaders followed.

These then are the five defining features of the new politics—radicalism, liberalism, faith in the potentialities of American democracy, predominant reliance on peaceful tactics for achieving political goals, and determination to supplant the politics of candidates with a politics of issues. Taken individually, none of these defining features is new. Taken collectively and implanted in a fast-growing segment of the American public, they astound and confound the forces that frustrate America's prospects for a liberal future. Hope is renewed that America will yet redeem the promise of a good life for every citizen; that it will yet become a force, not for war and counterrevolution, but for peace and justice throughout the world.

ARNOLD S. KAUFMAN

November 15, 1969

PREFACE TO THE FIRST EDITION

Convulsions in the world produce reverberations within political groups and movements. Social disorder and official reactions to disorder have resulted in deepening division within the ranks of American liberalism. Whether the turbulence is in Vietnam or the Dominican Republic, in Watts or Atlanta, Berkeley or the University of Michigan, liberals disagree sharply among themselves about causes and remedies. Indeed, often the most reflective and determined opposition to action by officials who think of themselves as liberals comes from others who also regard themselves as liberals. Controversy about American policy in Vietnam is, of course, the most dramatic instance of this development.

In the circumstances it is not surprising that millions of liberals are, and know they are, deeply confused about what to think and do politically. My aim has been to articulate one perspective in terms of which answers to the problems that beset liberals can be sought and found—a point of view that is rooted in liberalism's main intellectual and moral tradition—the tradition of John Stuart Mill, Leonard Hobhouse, and John Dewey.

The scheme of the book is simple. I first state what lies at the heart of liberalism as I construe the tradition (Chapter 1). I then argue that, viewed from the moral perspective described, chronic social ills in American society are so great that one cannot be authentically liberal unless he is radical (Chapter 2). An analysis of two defective political styles—the politics of pseudo-realism and self-indulgence—follows. I argue that both political tendencies sacrifice effectiveness; the first because it stresses political results too much, the second because it does not emphasize results enough (Chapters 3 and 4). The analysis and criticism of these defective political styles leads to a statement of the theory of democracy and of the strategic principles liberals ought to adopt (Chapter 5). In the last three chapters I apply the results of what has gone before to problems that have produced the disorder that today most agitates liberals—civil rights, higher education, and foreign policy. For the problems that arise in connection with each of these issues have most fully exposed American liberalism's internal divisions to public view.

I want to make it clear that the arguments of this book, especially those that describe the moral underpinnings of the conclusions drawn, are not fully developed. My aim has been to write a political tract the analyses and results of which rest on secure philosophical and moral foundations. I am presently working on another book which will develop those foundations in much greater detail.

My principal aim throughout has been to suggest how the gap between liberal rhetoric and liberal action can be closed without unacceptable loss of political effectiveness.

The inclination to write this book grew out of my participation in the teach-in movement and in the civil rights struggle. The idea was born while I was helping to organize the National Teach-In in May 1965. The initial draft was completed while I was teaching at the Tuskegee Institute in Alabama.

Many friends, colleagues, and students have helped to shape the ideas developed in this book. But my main debts are to Henry David Aiken, Frithjof Bergmann, Richard Boyd, Cortland Cox, Irving Howe, Thomas Robischon, Albert Wheeler, and Richard Wasserstrom. Sometimes opposing, sometimes supporting and helping to develop my thinking on various topics, each has given something to me for which I am grateful. I also thank Mrs. H. L. Joyner, Mrs. Alice Gantt, and Miss Lois Addison, each of whom contributed with remarkably good temper to the preparation of the manuscript.

Finally, I thank my wife who read countless drafts, made countless suggestions, and was determined that the final draft should be clear and well-written—often in the face of an impatience on the part of the author that might have caused someone less persistent to yield ground for the sake of peace. Any good writing that there may be in this book I owe to her.

ARNOLD S. KAUFMAN

March 1967

Many religious exercises are entered into with seeming fervour, where the heart, at the time, feels cold and languid: A habit of dissimulation is by degrees contracted: And fraud and falsehood become the predominant principle.

DAVID HUME

If he is to think politically in a realistic way, the intellectual must constantly know his own social position. This is necessary in order that he may be aware of the sphere of strategy that is really open to his influence. If he forgets this, his thinking may exceed his sphere of strategy so far as to make impossible any translation of his thought into action, his own or that of others. His thought may become fantastic. If he remembers his powerlessness too well, assumes that his sphere of strategy is restricted to the point of impotence, then his thought may easily become politically trivial. In either case, fantasy and powerlessness may well be the lot of his mind.

C. WRIGHT MILLS

1 LIBERALISM AND ITS DILEMMAS

Seldom have American liberals been so feverishly divided about anything as they are today about the Administration's Vietnam policies. The rough consensus that liberals had arrived at on both domestic and foreign policy issues has been rudely shattered by the reverberations of this war.

It would be a mistake to suppose that this rift is an isolated case—an accident of shifting political events. Rather, the growing disagreement among liberals is a dramatic symptom of latent differences that have too long been obscured by consensus-making rhetoric. The previously dormant issues are fundamental. For they include questions about the nature and function of democracy, the nature and actual threat of Communism, and the political strategies that best serve liberal aims.

Liberals have been too preoccupied with their internal

conflict, too shocked by its intensity, to have spent much time trying to articulate the bases of disagreement as clearly and comprehensively as the task deserves. The critics of American liberalism have, by contrast, been actively analyzing and attacking. Both Right and Left accuse liberals of being self-deluded, weak-willed, and pusillanimous. But where the Right maintains that liberal cowardice consists of being soft on Communism, the Left holds that its weakness consists in fearful deference to the metaphysicians of the Cold War. The Right views liberals as leading America down the road to serfdom; the Left as permitting America's fate to be determined by corporate elites whose exclusive concern is with protection of vested interests. Yet both criticisms fail, though not in equal measure, because neither set of critics is capable of seeing that the present crisis of American liberalism is due primarily to liberalism's failure properly to exploit its own traditional resources. For the liberal tradition possesses moral and intellectual resources richer than those of any competing tradition. The Right fails to acknowledge this because it rejects or distorts that tradition; the Left fails because, in its passion for a new revolutionary rhetoric, it blinds itself to the radical implications of liberalism's very old aims and principles.

The Flight from Reason

Too many liberals respond to their critics by splitting the difference. They balance the "extremist radicalism" of the Right against the "extremist radicalism" of the Left, and congratulate themselves for displaying intelligence and moral acumen. But "extremism" is not a matter of radical policies. Extremism is essentially an abuse of the traditions of reason and civility.

Liberals themselves participate in extremist politics so

conceived. Their participation is expressed in two deranged forms of political life—the politics of pseudo-realism and the politics of self-indulgence. The former is rooted in the belief that political action in pursuit of goals that are not "possible" or "practical" is irrational. The latter, in the belief that political action that does not express to the full a person's "authentic" moral feelings is insincere and immoral.

The concept of "realism" involved in the first is defective; the form of "authenticity" involved in the second is spurious. The politics of pseudo-realism cuts the nerve of action; the politics of self-indulgence impedes effective action. Though pseudo-realism grows out of cupidity, ambition, fear, prudence, a tendency to moral masochism, lack of compassion, and weariness, it is nourished by defective commitment to the traditions of reason. And though self-indulgence is promoted by passionate moral commitment, frustration, moral outrage, romantic exuberance, and generational mistrust, it too is nourished by defective commitment to the traditions of reason.

In this essay I will examine in detail both of these political styles. For an important burden of my argument is to show that the defects of contemporary American liberalism are due in the main to a breakdown in the institutions of reason. The analysis will proceed on the basis of caricature: idealized profiles that describe no individual perfectly. This method is justified on the grounds that these composite profiles do identify important and coherent tendencies that anyone familiar with the contemporary American political scene should have little difficulty in recognizing.

But the main burden of my argument is to show that liberalism's survival as a vital force in American politics depends on a resolute turn toward radicalism. For if unreason is the main defect of those who practice the politics of self-indulgence, the serious moral concern and desire to live authentically that make them radical are conditions also of authentic liberalism.

The Heart of Liberalism

Liberalism is a political theory, and therefore provides a guide to the making of public policy. All liberals share the belief that the ultimate aim of public policy is the protection and promotion of each person's equal opportunity to develop his potentialities as fully as possible. The limits of possibility for the individual are partly set by unalterable biological, physical, and social circumstances. But additional moral limits are set by the constraints of civility—those traits of character that make possible stability, mutual trust, collective regard for human welfare, and justice in the organization of society.

These convictions, though basic, are not distinctive to liberalism. A Marxist who is also a humanist could accept them. A liberal and such a Marxist would, however, normally disagree in two fundamental ways.

Marxists have always tended to be more optimistic than liberals about the possibility of transforming the social order in ways that will eliminate the need for organized reliance on instruments of force and violence. Expressed in the doctrine of "the withering away of the state," Marxists have traditionally tended to accept the view that neither self-regarding nor antisocial traits are indelibly etched in human beings. They have supposed that these traits can be erased by the right sort of social environment. Whether crossed by Hobbes, Freud, Niebuhr, or Sartre, liberals typically range from cautious skepticism to outright pessimism about the prospect of achieving that final alteration in the human constitution necessary to transform man's earthly condition into a veritable heaven of warm-hearted relationships.

Nevertheless, disagreement in this respect is one of emphasis—and increasingly so. For responsible Marxists, especially those in countries where Communism has assumed power, are fast revising their views on this point. The evident need to deal with economic inefficiency by reintroducing competitive market mechanisms has compelled them to acknowledge, in practice at least, the psychological truth on which adherence to the market mechanism has been traditionally based: that in any social situation normal persons are, to some extent, incorrigibly acquisitive.

The second disagreement is more definite and intractable than the first. Marxists believe that by eliminating what they call "the alienation of labor" all the other chronic ills of society that are remediable will also disappear. This *principle of the sufficiency of unalienated labor* requires the elimination of two conditions that, for the Marxist, constitute alienation of labor: the unjust distribution of the products of work and the stultifying character of the conditions of work.

Liberals may argue about how we are to understand "distributive justice," but otherwise they agree with the Marxist's moral assessment of the alienation of labor. Liberals do not, however, accept the principle of the sufficiency of unalienated labor. For they do not share the Marxist's belief that all the chronic and remediable ills of society will disappear once the alienation of labor has been ended. In particular, liberals are convinced that political democracy, by which they *at least* mean the right of any group to organize political opposition to existing power, is independent of alienation of labor, and just as basic to the realization of a good society. They believe that those who are opposed to existing institutional arrangements should normally have the fullest possible freedom to contest prevailing power by spreading alternative aims and programs before the public. Liberals concede that political democracy is not always desirable; for, as John Stuart Mill emphasized in *Representative Government*, there are cultural and economic prerequisites of formal democracy. But where these prerequisites do not exist, society should be so organized as to develop them as rapidly as possible. And this requires that a *liberal* case against complete freedom to speak, to publish, and to organize be established with absolute decisiveness before any departure from maximum freedom can be regarded as morally permissible. Liberals may no longer agree with Lord Acton's claim that "Power corrupts, and absolute power corrupts absolutely"; but they are convinced that even benevolent power is used manipulatively, and that absolute power tends to be used to manipulate absolutely. Increasingly it is manipulation rather than the naked exercise of power that poses the greatest threat to liberal institutions.

Here we come to the two ideals that most people regard as distinctive of liberalism: liberty and rational choice. Authentic liberalism implies that the cherished fulfillment of human potentialities can only be achieved through *self-fulfillment*. Moreover, formal liberty to live according to unreflective preference will not suffice. The choices must also be made thoughtfully. In a brief sentence, liberals believe that *a good society is one in which each person possesses the resources of materials, mind, and spirit, as well as the opportunities, to carve out a career in conformity to that person's own nature and reasoned choice.*

If a liberal is a utilitarian, he regards these resources and the freedom to utilize them as essential conditions of a satisfying life. But many liberals also regard freedom as intrinsically valuable, perhaps even divinely endowed with value. Metaphysical differences of this sort are philosophically but not politically important. For the different beliefs are consistent with the core of liberal conviction that I have tried to articulate.

This is not the place to develop in detail the implications of this doctrine. Nevertheless, the liberal attitudes toward democracy and the welfare state require special discussion because they provide the focus for much left-wing criticism of American liberalism.

Liberal emphasis on the importance of liberty and human rights, and the corresponding sensitivity to the danger of tyrannical abuse of corporate power, has resulted in an insistence on the fundamental value of political democracy. As I argued, this conviction marks the most important difference between liberalism and Marxist humanism. Yet the conviction has in many ways been the soft underbelly of the liberal position. For, too often, in "bourgeois" society formal democracy *has* been "the talking shop" that Marx claimed it was. Parliamentary institutions have been used by vested power to shape the form of policy in manipulatively appealing ways, without affecting its substance. And even when political democracy functions constructively, it is far from providing the panacea for social evils that many like to think it does.

Expression of disdain for political democracy by many on the Left is, therefore, quite understandable. Indeed, we need more, not less, legitimate criticism of the way in which men who are profoundly undemocratic in spirit and action use the instruments of formal democracy to manipulate consensus about matters with respect to which no one can reasonably expect consensus. The time is long overdue for liberals to attack those who, on the pretext of calling the faithful to reason together, use the occasion to manipulate and mesmerize opposition.

But criticism from the Left which proclaims commitment to "participatory democracy" and disdain for American liberalism in the same breath is ironical. For the need to deepen and enrich the quality of the democratic process, to make it both more deliberative and more participatory, flows directly from the central doctrines of liberalism as I have stated them. Those who proclaim their transcendental commitment to democracy in attacking the liberal tradition have either not read, or not understood, Rousseau,* John Stuart Mill, L. T. Hobhouse, or John Dewey—to mention but a few of the major liberal theorists.

* I know there are many who will object to this characterization of Rousseau. Here I can only say that Rousseau's masterwork, the *Social Contract*, is one of the most misread and, consequently, abused books in the history of political philosophy.

On the other hand, a person who views democracy exclusively in terms of a system of countervailing powers fails to understand that stability and protection against tyranny are neither the only functions of democracy nor always the most important. At least equally important is provision of the institutional soil which nourishes these very tendencies, sentiments, and powers of mind that enable a person both deliberatively to carve out his career and to play a responsible role in shaping social policies that vitally affect his life. To this extent, the proper charge against uncritical admirers of a conception of democracy conceived exclusively as a way to maintain a delicately balanced system of competing powers is not that they are too liberal but that they have lost touch with the very core of liberalism. Few are more guilty of fostering the illiberal preference for a countervailing power conception of democracy than those liberals who practice the politics of pseudo-realism—a point that will subsequently be developed.

It is easy, however, to exaggerate this criticism of the liberal realist's conception of democracy. For if a conception of countervailing power is not the whole of a liberal theory of democracy, it is at least an essential part. It is difficult to see how, in the long run, a more participatory and deliberative conception of democracy can be made to function effectively except by preparing the ground for its growth through a system of coalition politics. In such a system the inherent instability of the main coalitions permits both movement and that degree of general social stability without which chaos or revolution would result. Moreover, only within a structure that institutionalizes the competition for power can the tendency to use the instruments of a participatory democracy in manipulative ways be effectively countered—as Yugoslavia's quite remarkable experiment with workers' councils is beginning to make clear. As these points go to the heart of my criticism of many who practice the politics of self-indulgence, I will develop the argument more fully later. In regard to welfare programs, liberal realists and those who practice the politics of self-indulgence make mistakes that parallel their defective ideas about democracy. The realists exaggerate the virtues of the welfare state; some in the New Left underestimate both its accomplishments and its potentials.

Too many liberals sincerely justify a structure of welfare institutions that undermines a person's sense of responsibility, his dignity, and his freedom to make his own choices. Whether expressed as a reform theory of punishment or as a therapeutic theory of social services, there is too much tendency to coerce and manipulate "clients" for their own good. I see no essential moral difference between a rapidly growing social work profession guided by the notion that it is proper to compel or induce persons to accept therapeutically sound life goals, and a Big Brotherly effort to shape the inner life of citizens so that they come to prefer conformity over dissent, regardless of where the weight of morality and reason may lie.

From these remarks it does not follow that the accomplishments of welfare politics are negligible. Perhaps the ability to realize unsound "bourgeois" preferences is part of the price that must be paid for that minimal level of cradle-to-grave economic security without which the very possibility of a transmutation of values can not be achieved. If so, it is a price that should be paid. The unrestrained denunciation of the accomplishments of the welfare state that has become increasingly common among many on the "New Left" is an arrogance, a piece of cultural snobbery, that must be criticized and fought by genuine liberals.

The Limits of Politics

To sum up, liberals aim at conditions that permit and encourage every person to develop his potentialities as fully as possible. This can happen only when efforts to shape both career and public policy are controlled by the disciplines of reason. For liberals, complete freedom is the indispensable condition of these goals—qualified only by the moral and prudential constraints of civility, and of liberalism itself. They believe that except for societies in which the cultural and economic prerequisites of democracy have not been achieved, parliamentary institutions are required. And even in the former, the growing points of parliamentary institutions must be steadily created and consolidated. But participatory democracy is both an outcome and, I would here add, a condition of the more "formal" democracy of countervailing coalitions. For no society can pull itself up by its bootstraps. Just as it needs accumulations of capital to fuel its economic growth, so it needs accumulations of the essential traits of the responsible citizen to fuel its political growth. And how are such traits to be acquired without the sustained experience of taking responsibility?

While chary of those who view welfare benefits as a means of manipulating the "needy" into some "therapist's" version of the good life, or into political quiescence, liberals recognize that such benefits are hard-won, valuable concessions wrung at great cost from those who have clung to privilege. Liberals are, therefore, committed to the task of completing the work of the welfare state, even as they move politically to cope with some of the basic disorders of social life, the remedies for which may finally lie beyond the welfare state.

A critic of liberalism may point out the lack of any emphasis on fraternity, community, fellowship in the account I have given. The liberal may properly reply that he has always believed that, to the extent that satisfactory human relationships are possible, their realization depends on the existence of persons who possess dignity, self-esteem, and the cultural and industrial resources required to lead productive and meaningful lives. If society is arranged so that these qualities and resources are possessed by the maximum number of persons possible, then we have done all that can be done *through politics* to satisfy the aspirations people have for communion and salvation.

Implicit in this last remark is a very important thesis—one that has always been inherent in liberal theory. *Politics is limited.* Those who seek to fulfill apocalyptic visions through political activity are bound to become disillusioned. If Calvin, Hobbes, or Freud are correct in their descriptions of human nature, the salvation sought is beyond our worldly reach. Even if pessimistic accounts of human nature are mistaken, there is a sphere of personal struggle and aspiration that one may never be able to affect through the control of the crude levers of power with which political groups must ultimately be content. The realization that this is so is at once the end of innocence and the beginning of effectiveness in the pursuit of legitimate social goals.

2 THE NEED
FOR A TURN
TOWARD
RADICALISM

The United States is the representative industrial nation; a harbinger of what nations taking their first, halting steps toward full industrialization may expect—and a warning. Though we have achieved a degree of material affluence that boggles the imagination, the moral and aesthetic costs have often been too high.

The magnitude of American wealth and power has made certain ideals feasible goals of public policy. The President who proclaimed a war on national poverty yesterday proclaims a war on world hunger today. He announces that this country's mission is to defend freedom around the globe. Freedom, he reminds us, is indivisible. But if his actions are any test of actual intentions, he really does not mean it. For the War on Poverty was financially skimpy and politically hamstrung from the start. Success in the war on hunger will require vastly more than the convenient emptying of the granaries holding America's immense agricultural surpluses. And the sincerity of our defense of freedom is rendered somewhat more than doubtful by our actions in Vietnam and the Dominican Republic—to mention only two outrages in the conduct of American foreign policy.

The point I am making is this: We seem to have entered a political era in which the rhetoric of liberalism is unrestrainedly used either to defend programs of liberal reform that are minimal in magnitude and scope, or to rationalize programs that are illiberal in spirit and intent. In so doing, the present Administration is merely carrying to its most extravagant conclusion a misuse of the rhetoric of liberalism in which every political leader has to some extent participated. Increasingly, Administrations have tended to substitute liberal rhetoric for liberal policy in an effort to allay discontent without risking substantial change. But the strategy will not work for reasons that are entirely out of the control of any American government, except one genuinely prepared to match radical deed to radical word.

The Dialectic of Disorder

There is a dialectic of disorder at work in the world. It is a dialectic every bit as ruthless in its impact on human hopes and values as any Hegel ever dreamed of. It spares no society, and few people. It is impartial in the way it defeats the plans of both dropouts and Presidents. And the misuse of the rhetoric of liberalism has contributed in no small measure to the operation of that dialectic.

For even empty rhetoric generates aspirations among people who take it seriously. Aspirations kindle new and concrete hopes. But then the emptiness of the rhetoric is revealed in the paucity and perversion of the implementing programs. Thus expectations are not fulfilled, and frustration and bitter anger result. The expression of this anger differs, depending on the intensity of the expectations and the extent of the gap between program and fulfillment. In the ghettoes of Newark and Detroit there are bloody riots. At Berkeley there are all-night sit-ins and "filthy speech." At Michigan, teach-ins. In Mississippi, an attempt is made to take over an air base. And America's Catholic hierarchy encounters the most exasperating challenge to its authority from subordinate priests and laymen with which it has ever had to deal.

But the dialectic of disorder that results from the gap between rhetoric and practice in the United States is as nothing when compared with the ferocious consequences of frustrated expectations and revolutionary action abroad. In Vietnam, the Dominican Republic, Indonesia, in Venezuela, Bolivia, and Nigeria, in Syria, the Congo, and Yemen, men and women touched by hope and expectation for the first time in their lives, for the first time in the lives of generations, are plunged into open and bloody rebellion. But our leaders seem to understand the one no better than the other. The Sheriff Clark who terrorizes children is but a step removed from Chief Parker who believes that the only way to deal with the rioters of Watts is to beat them over the head. And he in turn is but a step away from the President who, despite all his disclaimers, places his faith mainly in napalm and rockets. What price freedom? Approximately nine noncombatants and $375,000 per Viet Cong dead.* I am sure that each of these men must, in a quiet moment, suffer nausea at the things they "must" authorize. They are as much victims as oppressors. And they do differ substantially in their moral outlook. But they have in common an inability to understand the dialectic of disorder; and a consequent

* Bernard B. Fall, "And Still the Little Men of the Vietcong Keep Coming," *The New York Times Magazine*, March 6, 1966, p. 21. A. D. Borchgrave, "Then and Now—The Difference," *Newsweek*, March 14, 1966, p. 41.

tendency to cope with disorder by beating people over the head.

Equally important—they mistake political quiescence for joy. Before the Montgomery bus boycott the entire segregationist population of the South had deluded itself into believing that the "darkies" were content with their lot. One Southern segregationist recently echoed that mood unwittingly when he wistfully complained that he could not understand why "the niggers ain't singing anymore." This victim of Southern racism is unable to understand that, when one cannot hope, there is little to do but mask misery and terror with song. But once hope is kindled, the songs end, the dialectic of disorder begins, and, before long, disorderly process is converted into insistent political pressure.

Thus, if liberal rhetoric does breed anger and discord, it also generates hope and political movement. This at least is to the good. For the time is brought closer when American liberals will reclaim their rhetoric and put it firmly back into the service of radical change. Confronted by the sordid reality of American affluence, it is impossible for someone to be authentically liberal without turning resolutely toward radicalism. Thus, to the extent that the rhetoric of political leaders encourages sincere commitment to liberalism, it also fosters opposition to the illiberal allocation of America's vast resources, and to the illiberal use of America's vast power.

The time must come when the recitation of past liberal achievements no longer tranquilizes American liberals. For scrutiny of the present state of American society discovers a reality that is at least as outrageous as it is full of products and promise.

The Distribution of Wealth

The United States is economically one of the most unequal societies in the world, and the most affluent. The fifth of the nation that is poverty-stricken gives the lie to any claim that we have learned how to manage our affluence in a humanly acceptable way.

The very magnitude of our national resources makes it possible to maintain an adequate incentive system, and still meet all the functional needs generated by the moral pre-eminence of personal self-development in the liberal scheme of things. Ironically, just when Communist nations are discovering that they must reintroduce sharper material incentives, the United States is in a position to reverse the emphasis traditionally placed on them.

Increasingly, the most important incentives are the quality of the conditions of work and the value the individual places on the products of his labor. It is clear that the main barriers to redistribution are not those that flow from the requirements of continued economic growth, but the entrenched power of moneyed elites who, either out of habit or acquisitiveness, insist on interpreting the rhetoric of American freedom in the least human way possible. These forces are often unwittingly abetted by good-hearted folk who are willing to accept the first, tiny product of massive legislative effort as sufficient because it is so beguilingly packaged by the Great Society.

For the indefinite future, the problems of redistribution are going to be complicated by the technological revolution that is in process. The long-term prospect is steady attrition in the supply of jobs. Thus, the nation is conditioned to accept as a triumph of political statesmanship a rate of unemployment that a humane society should not tolerate.

The dialectic of disorder operates with increasing ferocity in this area. Rent strikes, a rising crime rate, intensified problems of juvenile delinquency, and the growth of general contempt for formal authority are only a few of the by-products of the growing gap between the rhetoric of affluence and the reality of poverty. And these disorders are increasingly independent of the problem of race.

Civil Rights

The United States is still a predominantly racist society. Economically, socially, legally, politically and, perhaps most important of all, educationally, we have eliminated many legal barriers, yet have made little progress in fact. In comparison with fifteen years ago, Negroes are more segregated, receive a smaller proportion of the national income, constitute a higher proportion of the unemployed, the under-educated, and the blue-collar work force. The only area in which Negroes appear to have made massive gains during the last decade and a half is in the proportion of wartime casualties they are constrained to accept. For in the Vietnam War, over 14 per cent of the combatants and 18 per cent of the casualties are Negro soldiers, though only about 10 per cent of the total population is Negro.* Thus we are confronted by the supreme moral irony; those who share least in the fruits of American freedom are, in its alleged defense, making the supreme sacrifice proportionately more of the time than those who benefit most.

The white majority and its allies within the Negro middle class are oblivious to these facts. They are all too ready to accept the tokens of political appointment, the forms of a changing legal code, the apparent moderation of more virulent racial attitudes, and the promise of presidential rhetoric for the substance of significant change. But though there may háve been substantial progress for a small proportion of lucky Negroes, the great bulk of the 20 million Negroes in America have participated in this progress only to the extent

* It is true that many of the Negroes in combat in Vietnam are formally volunteers. But when they can escape from the black belt of the South or the ghettoes of the North only by enlisting in the Army, then we have compulsion. As one VISTA worker in Alabama told me recently, many young Negroes he encountered were happy to be accepted by the Armed forces. But their motive was escape, not patriotism.

that their expectations have risen without a proportionate increase in the relative extent to which those expectations are satisfied.

Twelve years after the school desegregation decision, 95 per cent of Southern schools are segregated. Though unemployment for all groups is down, the rate of Negro unemployment relative to whites is rising. Since 1955, in Alabama, 20 persons have been murdered in circumstances growing out of the civil rights movement, and no one has to date been convicted for any of these crimes. In Harlem the mortality rate at birth for Negroes is currently 45 per 1,000; for the total New York City population, including the Negroes of Harlem, about 25 per 1,000. In Mississippi the median income for Negroes is 32 per cent of the median income for whites. These are but a few of the large number of facts that dramatize the gap between what Negroes have been promised and what they have actually received. A white majority, spoon-fed facts that largely point to progress in civil rights, is then utterly astonished by violence in Watts or Rochester.

This white majority and its Negro allies then grow impatient at the rising tempo of demonstrations, violence, and threatened violence by Negroes. The characteristic reaction of officialdom, whether in Selma or in Watts, is to club the incorrigibles into submission. In no other phase of domestic life, however, does the dialectic of disorder work with such ruthless efficiency to destroy the illusions of those "decent and respectable" Americans who stand ready to do anything —anything at all—to improve human relations—except to contemplate seriously the necessity of relinquishing many of their basic social and economic prerogatives.

Education

The Groves of Academe are increasingly the scene of guerilla warfare. Sit-ins, teach-ins, demonstrations, filthy-speech, and

teachers' strikes—all are the products of the same fundamental disorders of American education. Disorderly process in
our schools, a source of so much perplexity to most, is not
difficult to understand from the point of view of liberalism.

For education, more than any other process, is essential to
the achievement of a society in which persons carve out their
destiny according to their natures and their own deliberative
choices. It is in our schools that the traditions of reason
should be honored and cultivated, the power of the human
agent to live authentically and autonomously celebrated and
encouraged. And in large measure reason is honored, autonomy is celebrated. But the prevailing rhetoric is not translated into educational policy. Quite the reverse; the actual
trend of developments makes more and more difficult the
achievement of promised goals. The Socratic ideal of the
examined life gives way to an educational process that rewards
academic imperialism, fits individuals to socially needed
functional slots, and, by means of paternal manipulation,
adapts students for that conformity to the conventional wisdom which a society devoted to consensus and minimal dis-
turbance of the social order requires.

But academic administrators, no more than political
leaders, can escape the impact of the dialectic of disorder.
Youngsters who are promised one thing, given another, and
provided with enough of the intellectual and moral resources
to realize that they have been defrauded, will, at least oc-
casionally, take it out on the "system." And well they should.

Disraeli's aphorism, "Any man who is not a radical in his
twenties lacks a heart, while any man who remains a radical
after thirty lacks a head," is, in its application to the United
States, only half right. The tragedy of student radicalism is
not that it exists, but that it so quickly atrophies. How could
it be otherwise? Student radicals have been deprived to the
same extent as their more conservative contemporaries of
systematic training in the disciplines of reason and of exposure to morally serious models whose notion of "responsi-

bility" does not preclude radical dissent. No group in higher education is more massively victimized than undergraduates —who suffer most from the inverted system of priorities that rewards organizational skills more than research, research more than graduate teaching, graduate teaching more than undergraduate teaching, the teaching of undergraduate honor students more than the teaching of those whose need for skilled and dedicated teachers is greatest.

If life in the multiversity is too often fraudulent, it at least provides the increasingly essential passport to the fulfillment of those more material aspirations that American society encourages one to have. Hence, the fact that millions are excluded from the privileges of higher education for economic reasons alone is doubly scandalous. Not only are these persons deprived of even the illusion of participating in what is promised by American rhetoric, they are also excluded from the material opportunities necessary to participate in the reality of commercial success. And even when opportunities are available, inadequate early education deprives millions of others of developing either the motivation or the necessary skills for achieving what is conventionally termed "success" in more advanced schooling.

This is not to deny that the United States is doing better than most in educating youth. But for a nation possessing our resources, today's best is at least a light-year away from being good enough. Thus, we have another American dilemma—bad educational processes, inequitably accessible, rationalized by an almost empty rhetoric of educational ideals.

Conditions of Work

Due primarily to industrial organization and the unprecedented period of relative prosperity this nation has enjoyed, since the beginning of World War II, the opportunity to exercise power arbitrarily has greatly diminished in our work-places. This abatement of industrial tyranny is due primarily to the creation of a system of industrial due process that, though far from being comprehensive, does protect most blue- and white-collar workers. This system of due process—and not rising wages and salaries—is trade unionism's major achievement. Ask any fairly sophisticated group of leaders from union locals, as I have done, and they will tell you that this is so.

But if due process is an achievement, and a historic agenda that remains to be completed, there is another problem that has hardly been perceived, let alone attacked. For though the workplace is not the theater of tyrannical exercise of power in its more blatant forms, (for example, sweat shops, company stores, Pinkertons, brutal foremen, etc., are gradually disappearing) it is the place where life is lived in its most routine, uncreative, spirit-searing—in a word, dehumanized—forms.

In an article in which he brilliantly analyzes the impact of modern industrial conditions on workers, Harvey Swados suggests that until workers acquire control of production standards, the very rules of the industrial game, no matter how impartially applied, will perpetuate and aggravate this dehumanizing aspect of the work process.* (Shades of early Marx.) For the company's primary concern is to increase profits. When wages, fringe benefits, and the more general conditions of work are rigidly prescribed by collective bargaining agreements, the competitive pressures with which the company will normally deal will force management to do one of two things: make technological improvements that eliminate jobs or speed up the work process. The threat of the former gives them a lever by which they can achieve the latter. The imperatives of speed-up require the elimination of all those "frictional" concessions that mitigate efficiency.

* Harvey Swados, "The UAW and Walter Reuther," *Dissent,* Autumn 1963.

Moreover, the very existence of due process removes the last reservation the conscientious manager might have about authorizing a speed-up. It actually permits him to treat the worker like a machine, with good conscience. For the worker has his contract and is guaranteed his day in court, should he disagree with the manager's application of its provisions. Doesn't he?

Once again the dialectic of disorder operates with a ruthless impartiality. Unless trade unions take appropriate steps, the day is coming when most strikes will be unofficial and directed not against employers but against labor leadership itself. For, in the very nature of the case, "responsible" union leadership "must" support employers in their legitimate application of contractual provisions and therefore often assist marginal producers to survive by stretching points in their favor, both during and after negotiations. But the rhetoric of the trade union movement proclaims that the trade union leader is a worker's best friend. Confronted by the gap between that rhetoric and the dehumanized reality of the work process, there will be disorder within the industrial community. And all the decent and respectable members of the professional middle class will decry the "irresponsibility" of the "greedy" workers.

Liberalism's course is clear. It must reinterpret and apply the moral insights of older syndicalist theorists of industrial democracy, like G. D. H. Cole and John Dewey. For in the industrial community, as in the larger political community, protection of human rights requires democratic process.

Legal Justice

If due process is close to having been realized in that part of industry which is organized, it is far from having been achieved within the formal structures of the law. The legal rights of the poor, of the Negroes, and of those who profess unpopular political creeds are still too often violated. This comes about partly through unequal administration of existing rules, but more often through the social prejudice that influences the very construction of rules of legal process.

Almost all executions are of persons that come from deprived backgrounds. Indigents rarely get adequate legal counsel; and when they do, they often obtain that counsel after their rights have already been violated in the pre-trial process. The Imbau method of interrogation, now widely used by police, is refined brain-washing. The drawing of juries and grand juries is often so contaminated by racial and social prejudice that there is little possibility of a fair trial. Standards of mitigation and criminal responsibility all favor the more socially respectable members of the community. And the severity of the sentences that American justices often hand out is an international scandal.

Conditions of penal servitude and rules of legal commitment frequently violate the most basic principles of liberalism. In the guise of *treatment*, the individual's basic right to freedom of choice, with all the fateful consequences for good and ill in his own life and in the life of society, is violated. Reform is all right when the process and aim are the development of the virtues of a free citizen, not when it masks an effort to manipulate the criminal or patient into conformity. In the guise of liberal reform, commitment to mental institutions has become a thoroughly illiberal device for getting obnoxious persons out of sight and under guard.

One is not less a manipulating tyrant if he makes his appearance as warden, psychiatrist, prison guard, hospital attendant, hospital administrator, or social worker. To no social evil is the basic thrust of liberal theory more definite and more important. For if, in the name of abstract justice, morally committed persons will not protect a person to whom family and neighbor are likely to be indifferent, who will?

It is, therefore, not enough to acknowledge real virtues in

the existing system of law, or the substantial progress that has been made in the last half century. Liberals must devise means of dealing with the extremely recalcitrant problems that remain.

Urban and Rural Life

As antiseptic suburbs grow, and the decay of central cities is accelerated by materialism, exhaust, and rapacious land-lords, the natural setting in which the dialectic of disorder can play itself out is created.

The problem of creating a decent physical environment for urban Americans has become so acute that the President has created the Department of Urban Affairs and has proposed a Department of Transportation. But no administrative gimmick, nor any of the Administration's current proposals for remedying the situation, has any prospect of correcting the basic problem—entrenched property interests that generally have the power to kill any decent measure of reform, and in pursuit of more profits almost invariably exercise that power in ways that subordinate or ignore considerations of aesthetics, health, and morality. Urban renewal is an anodyne that generally benefits middle-income groups more than lower-income people who are displaced by the public projects. Desegregation by law seems only to hasten segregation in fact in urban school districts. And the ugliness of the central city is mitigated only by the central city businessmen's efforts to lure the shopping-center crowd back through "beautifica-tion" of their surroundings.

Cumulative Impact

Liberalism is concerned not only that a person have freedom to do those things he prefers, but that what he prefers result from the fullest possible exposure to the existing range of possibilities. For only then can the freedom to choose in a deliberative way be assured. Only then can we have any reasonable assurance that choice is a fulfillment, and not a waste of a person's power.

Liberals must tread a delicate line between cultural authoritarianism and cultural liberation—but in the name of the latter they must criticize the cultural marketplace that so restricts choice that what exists today comes close to being a cultural wasteland. Those who have the time and money, and know where to look, can find the cultural products they are seeking. But most ordinary Americans with relatively educated tastes find that they are discriminated against in a most egregious fashion. Here, as always, commercial criteria conflict sharply with the deliberative and aesthetic criteria that mark the difference between amusement and intensely human experience.

This is not to say that any male with a Ph.D., gonads, and a masculine ego is incapable of enjoying half-nude women and Western bravado very much. But during any given evening, during any given hour, both he and his female counterpart should like at least to have the opportunity to taste aesthetically and intellectually more venturesome fare than is available on radio and television in most places. Yet, in the final analysis, it must be admitted that the debasement of taste in this country is not the primary responsibility of those who presently control the media of mass communication. With the best will in the world, and many active in the mass media have very good will, they are constrained by conditions of the market. Defiance would take greater social and financial courage than is normally allotted to businessmen. These conditions are the cumulative product of institutional derangements described in all that has preceded. If an individual's life were rich in other respects, he would normally neither need to escape by consuming debased cultural fare, nor suffer harm or loss if he did. It is against the background of dehumanization from cradle to grave that the provision of special cultural opportunities takes on special importance.

The impact of the conditions I have described on our cultural lives is bad; their cumulative effect on the texture of the whole of American life is disastrous. The gap between rhetoric and reality is so wide, the values actually operative so unrelated to biological, intellectual, and spiritual development in its fullest sense, that an authentically human existence for most Americans is an impossibility. Perhaps most disastrous of all is that the operative criteria of public esteem, on which one's self-esteem and self-respect are so dependent, are sufficiently remote from the rhetoric of morality, intellect, and aesthetics proclaimed on ceremonial occasions, that the very possibility of living a life of integrity is deeply eroded when it is not destroyed. This is the common experience of the sensitive youngsters an older generation does not permit itself to understand fully. Understanding would require these older persons to face the lies that have controlled and impoverished their own lives. An older person cannot normally be expected to admit this to himself. For error, persistently pursued, traps the human mind. The more fateful the error, the more complete the entrapment. And so human error normally enlarges itself. The parent who has guided the child mistakenly redoubles his effort to "bring the child to his senses." The President who has guided his nation mistakenly does the same. The fault must be made to lie elsewhere—for sanity's sake.

Our spiritual, educational, and political leaders celebrate "freedom"; but they too often mean "bend your knee to power and consensus." They proclaim "democracy"; but they too often mean submission to the existing structure of corporate power. They call for "honesty, truth, and morality"; but they too often practice deception, hypocrisy, and ruthless violation of the rights of others in "patriotic" pursuit of policy aims "vital to the national interest." They debase the quality of the democratic process and attribute what they do to "love of country."

Where once the basic power and prerogatives of privileged elites were maintained primarily through more naked exercise of power, reliance is increasingly placed instead on the effort to limit the mind's power rationally to understand public policy. The result is extremism on the Right, and manipulated consensus in the middle.

What can a person of the Left who values authenticity do in the light of such conditions except grow progressively alienated from our predominantly middle-class culture—and, quite incidentally, grow long fingernails and a beard?

"Be realistic," answer most American liberals.

3 THE
POLITICS
OF
PSEUDO-
REALISM

The best statement of this most "realistic solution" I have ever encountered appeared in a student editorial entitled "Students Must Choose Between Politics and Ideals":

> Politics is the art of the possible. This is always a difficult adage for students, largely involved in one sort of political idealism or another, to accept. The "student movement" has lost sight of it. But if students expect to exert influence of any kind in society, they must accept it and realize that if what they want is the "impossible," they must find means outside the established political order to implement it.
>
> Politics must be accepted for what it is—amoral. Students would either have to compromise their ideals in order to participate or forget about participation. There is no reason to assume that student participation in the governmental processes would substantially alter the character of the American government.

> Students are double-damned. If they participate in politics, idealism of necessity goes out the window. If they do not enter the larger political sphere, they find that large and vital areas of concern, such as the future of the human race, are outside their scope. They must choose.

Out of the mouths of babes come the deranged teachings of their fathers. The author poses a cruel dilemma. Happily, it is also a false dilemma. To understand why the dilemma is false and why the preferred alternative of political realism is unacceptable, a philosophical exploration of the very bases of political thought and action is required.

From student editorial to Aristotle. The ascent is steep, but the path direct. For Aristotle, the supreme rational conservative, provides the clearest possible statement of realism's vital principle. "We deliberate about things that are in our power and can be done." And that is all we do, or even can deliberate about. Aristotle was so deeply committed to this principle that it shaped the very sense "deliberation" had for him. His meaning is clear; even the attempt to determine how to achieve an impossible object is a defect of intellect so gross that the thought processes involved do not merit the name, "deliberation." But two questions must be answered: How is one to determine what is, or is not, impossible? And what is the relationship between the belief that some object is impossible, and the likelihood that it will not be achieved?

The realist's answer to both questions is clear. The facts, scientifically established, reveal what is possible and what is not. The Gradgrind of political life, the realist proclaims, ". . . we want nothing but Facts, sir, nothing but Facts!" And, as facts are "out there," waiting to be discovered by inquiring intellect, what a man believes to be possible is not relevant to whether or not it is possible.

Aristotle crossed by the spirit of science; what could provide a more respectable intellectual façade for determined opposition to radical change? Science is a form of life. And like all other forms of life, it is, as Freud once said (and then forgot), governed "by deep-rooted internal prejudices, into whose hands our speculation unwittingly plays." In politics, the rhetoric of science no more guarantees moral rectitude, or even strategic acumen, than the rhetoric of Christian morality guarantees a righteous cause or good heart.

This holds no less for the liberal realist than the conservative realist. The liberal realist's criteria for assessing "the facts" and his very perception of "fact" are unwittingly governed by deep-rooted internal prejudices. He does not consciously betray his liberal commitments. Indeed, he possesses a most ingenious arsenal of defensive forms for masking his betrayal from himself. The two that deserve special mention are role-playing, and the view that politics is an amoral enterprise.

Role-Playing and Anticipatory Surrender

The role-player assumes that he is somehow not meeting his obligations as a responsible citizen unless, before making a political judgment, he views matters *as if* he were the official who has the formal power to act. This he does, not simply to understand and sympathize, but because he regards role-playing as required by the dictum that only deliberation about possibilities is warranted. If, from the President's point of view, a certain course of action is impossible, the role-player would think it deeply irresponsible for anyone to press the President to take that action.

For example, a really massive War on Poverty, involving expenditures of $100 billion over a five-year period, is under consideration. The role-player asks, "Can he get the legislation through the Congress?" If not, then he concludes that it is irresponsible for liberals to press for such a program.

Secretary of State Dean Rusk recently urged role-playing when considering the Vietnam issue. At a hearing held by the Senate Foreign Relations Committee he advised every

American to ask himself, "What would I do about this if I were President of the United States?"—and to make his political judgment on that basis. I can think of no advice which reflects a more defective understanding of the nature of responsible citizenship in a democracy.

For the policies endorsed by officials, from President down to the lowest policy-making levels, are almost invariably the product of a great many different, often conflicting, pressures. A person who role-plays by putting himself in the place of men at the center of power, in effect abandons any effort to make his special concerns and interests a part of the system of pressures that help shape the official's decision. Hence, members of groups who tend to role-play are, in effect, canceling any influence on policy they might exert. It is this tendency to role-play that has helped make authentic liberalism an increasingly peripheral force in American politics.

The most direct result of role-playing is anticipatory surrender of bargaining points. Since compromise is part of the art of politics, it requires a position forcefully articulated, persistently pressed, there to be compromised. Role-playing that results in anticipatory surrender will prove unrealistic. For the compromises made by officials will then almost inevitably be responsive only to pressures that have not been negated by anticipatory surrender—hence, the realist's pseudo-realism.

Rusk's counsel to the American people is the inversion of role-playing by an ordinary citizen. A responsible official who feels himself at the center of a system of forces tugging in different directions would normally welcome pressures that make it more possible for him to adopt a policy closer to his own, ideal preference. Thus, for example, if the President and his Secretary of State do want to reserve the right to negotiate the form of an interim South Vietnamese government at the bargaining table, they should welcome the proposal made by Senators J. William Fulbright and Robert

Kennedy that the National Liberation Front be granted a role in a governing coalition.* For this both increases the uncertainty about American intentions in the minds of the adversary and gives the Administration greater political freedom to compromise once it does sit down at the negotiating table. The fact that they react as if men like Senators Kennedy and Fulbright were stabbing them in the back will inevitably be interpreted by the adversary as good evidence that America's stated willingness to compromise on meaningful points is phony.

The process of identifying with the predicaments of others does have its uses. For, properly employed, it increases a person's political effectiveness by giving him a better sense of just where his limited power may be most effectively applied. Moreover, it diminishes those blaming-tendencies that so contaminate the capacity for detached political judgment—a vital condition of effectiveness. But empathy as a means of achieving maximum effectiveness should not be confused with role-playing.

The Amorality of Politics

The liberal realist tends to regard concern for the morality of political judgment and action as mere moralism. He tends to reserve his own invocation of moral principles for ceremonial occasions. In the councils of government, or of party, as journalist, educator, or man of God, he is the first to eschew the relevance of moral principle, the last to measure the propriety of the means in terms of anything other than their effectiveness in relation to "practical" goals. Morality is pertinent only in establishing a general goal as desirable. And in deciding questions of foreign policy, even this degree of

* Perhaps they do so privately. But all the evidence seems to indicate that they are more furious with their critics in private than in public.

morality is impermissible—the sole concern being for the national interest. The practicality of the goal and the effectiveness of means to that end are purely factual matters.

I have heard an ordained Presbyterian minister who happens to be a consultant to the Department of Defense argue that as a Christian he should not obey an order to fire nuclear weapons, but that his moral reservations are irrelevant to matters of policy because they require political, not moral, judgment.

The President betrayed a similar tendency when, commenting on recent Vietnam protests, he expressed surprise that "any person would feel toward his country in a way that is not consistent with the national interest."

I can think of no attitude more destructive of a civilized effort to cope with political problems. For these sentiments come out of the mouths, not always of cruel men, but often of morally sensitive officials who are the products of some of the best instruction our moral traditions make available. The attitude leads to an identification of national security with any national interest, and then to identification of national prestige with national security. Our young men are then committed to battle in a fruitless effort to forestall genuine social revolution rooted less in ideological commitment than in human misery resulting from decades of neglect and exploitation. The folly is then labeled "patriotism," and dissenters are accused of practicing "neo-isolationism" and "near treason." The path is precipitous and difficult to avoid once one has taken the first fateful step of construing politics as an amoral enterprise. When what the amoral view implies becomes clear, morally sensitive men are either driven into opposition, or go into an acquiescent state of moral shock.

It is tempting to criticize the realist's amorality as morally vicious, and to let matters go at that. In fact, even if one grants the amorality of politics, the view generates some of the deepest and most perplexing problems of political philosophy.

For one thing, the factual judgments made in support of political action almost inevitably go beyond the available evidence. This is so for two reasons: first, the amount of evidence that one may theoretically take into account is unlimited. But, more important, in political life, the actual evidence available is, as a rule, severely limited. Hence, factual judgments are made in conditions of indeterminacy in two different respects. Before developing the implications of the fact indeterminacy that exists for official and ordinary citizen alike, let me illustrate the claims, to fix their meaning more precisely.

Consider the factual judgment, "Communist China is an aggressive nation." What sorts of facts tend to confirm this statement? Well, there are the facts of actual Chinese military actions—against India, against Tibet, against Taiwan, against United States forces in Korea, against the off-shore islands. There are facts such as the ideology of revolution Chinese leaders profess. And there are speeches such as the famous one by Lin Piao. One could go on listing facts that tend to confirm the hypothesis of Chinese military aggressiveness. It is clear, however, that even if the evidence were unambiguous, there is always the possibility that embarrassing facts might turn up which go against the trend of evidence. Thus, many who thought they had enormous evidence for their belief that Russia was unalterably Stalinist in its basic institutional structure were astonished by Khrushchev's famous denunciation of Stalin. And many others who believed firmly that totalitarian societies are incapable of the creativity and "know-how" to develop advanced technology were shaken to their toes by Sputnik. Similar surprises may undermine current beliefs about China.

In fact, however, the state of the evidence for the hypothesis of Chinese aggressiveness is not nearly as clear as the catalogue alluded to above would suggest. China experts tell us that China has not, in fact, ever moved against territories with respect to which historic Chinese claims to sovereignty were not substantial. The sole exception is Korea; and there the presence of American military forces within sight of the Manchurian border could reasonably be viewed as an intolerable provocation. Lin's speech is interpreted differently by those who note that he does, after all, cautiously promise that China will give more vigorous support to wars of national liberation only "when we grow in strength as time goes on . . ."; which suggests that military intervention is not in prospect now, unless. . . . Moreover it is, after all, China that is encircled; and in the circumstances, a little defensive bellicosity is humanly to be expected. All this goes to prove not that China is benign but that the state of the evidence is at best indeterminate.

Given that for major judgments about facts in politics the evidence is almost always going to be incomplete, the beliefs on which a person finally settles are quite inevitably going to be governed "by deep-rooted internal prejudices"—by self-interest and ideological commitment. For if there is a gap between what is known and what is believed, then something besides what is known must have influenced what is believed. To think otherwise is self-deluding, and therefore irrational. Hence, the irony of the realist's position is that by worshiping fact he increases the probability that he will form beliefs irrationally. One who despises and fears Communism will selectively assess the evidence for the claim that China is aggressive, and *leap* to the conclusion that she is incorrigibly aggressive. By the same token, a realist who despises and fears "American imperialism" will selectively assess the evidence for the claim that the controlling principle of American foreign policy is counterrevolution.

The very language of fact is ideologically controlled. Consider the term "aggression." What does it mean? Is one country an aggressor against another when the first supplies training bases, logistical support, finances, armament, munitions, and some manpower to a group of nationals of another country so that they can more effectively fight the established government? Then both American action against Cuba at the time of the Bay of Pigs disaster, and North Vietnamese action against South Vietnam are acts of aggression. But if such support is not sufficient to constitute aggression, if the fighting force is predominantly indigenous to the country in which the fighting is taking place, then neither action constitutes aggression. This is why the United States *had* to propagate the myth that North Vietnamese were in the South in force prior to its escalation of the war. But how many who believe that North Vietnam is not an aggressor believe that the United States was? And how many "patriotic" Americans, who would deny that this country was an aggressor against Cuba, would passionately insist that we must defend the South Vietnamese because they have been the victims of aggression?

I was present one evening when a government official was asked whether he thought Communism was monolithically and unreservedly committed to the promotion of revolution everywhere. He replied, "Of course." Then he hesitated for a moment, and continued, "Except Yugoslavia; and she is not Communist at all." What's in a name? If the name is politically central enough, then an ideologue's most "deep-rooted internal prejudices" are bound to be in it. And, as there is no ideologue like a blind ideologue, realists, blinded as they are by their worship of fact, are the worst ideologues of all.

Moreover, to the extent that a realist's narrower interests tend to reinforce his fact-worship, he will have a double motive for concealing from himself the epistemological status of his fact judgments. But this is only to restate Marx's theory of class consciousness in an epistemologically relevant, nonideological way.

There is another point to be made here—one that has special appeal to radicals and special pertinence to the realist's maxim that one should pursue only what is possible. Regardless of how scrupulous factual inquiry leading to particular judgments may have been, to be limited in political aspiration only to what one believes can be achieved is more often than not to settle for less than one can achieve. William James made this point insistently and eloquently—and earned much abuse and misunderstanding for his trouble:

> Any philosophy which makes such questions as *What is the ideal type of community?* depend on the question of *What is going to succeed?* must needs fall back on personal belief as one of the ultimate conditions of the truth. For again and again success depends on energy of act, faith in turn on faith that we are right—which faith verifies itself.

I do not want to defend all the epistemological implications of this passage taken literally. What James is *at least* saying is that the likelihood that a goal will be achieved often depends on whether it is believed to be possible. "Faith" in the practicality of an aim is a condition of one's determination to pursue that aim, which is in turn an important condition of successful effort. Hence, the very rejection of a political goal as "impossible" or "impractical" or "unrealistic" tends to be a self-fulfilling prophecy. The difference between what is possible and what is impossible is often the will to believe.

James is suggesting an even more radical thesis—in both senses of the word "radical." He believed that one's very conception of "rationality" in political life, as in any other form of life, is in part shaped by temperament. The contrast between optimistic and pessimistic temperament pervades his work. It was his view that these "temperamental" factors cause the pessimist to reject as irrational risks that the optimist would accept as rational. In the application of this point, to political life at least, James seems to me to be indisputably correct. The radical, necessarily more optimistic about achieving a certain radical goal than the conservative, will tend to regard as a rational aim of political effort the goal which the conservative regards as irrational. But they may arrive at these different judgments on the basis of the same evidence. Not only fact but one's very conception of rationality may be influenced by ideology.

For all these reasons, even if one were to grant the realist's premise that morality ought to be irrelevant to political judgment, this would not make the moral point of view implicit in ideology irrelevant—because it cannot help but influence political judgment. The realist's dictum is itself a moral maxim that counsels us to accept a psychological impossibility—and it is therefore both unrealistic and a major source of irrationality in politics.

This point has special importance these days to those who proclaim the end of ideology. In the thirties many morally passionate young men were gulled into uncritical endorsement of various forms of Marxist ideology. With an arrogance whose magnificence is often overshadowed only by their egoism, they assume that if it happened to them in the thirties, it is likely to happen to anyone today. Thus, they set themselves up as the moral guardians of the present political generation—warning all against the insidious attractions of the gods that failed.

The most certain prophylaxis against mistaken commitment is, of course, absence of firm commitment. Hence, they proclaim the dangers of ideological thinking and the virtues of "the politics of the event." On almost every one of the fundamental political issues of our day they tend to reinforce conservatism and reaction in the name of liberalism. They exaggerate the rigidities of the Soviet system under Stalin, erode the determination to resist McCarthyism, strengthen those who condemn a sensitively moral response to United States adventures in foreign policy, side with those who defend the institutions of the bureaucratically stifling university, exaggerate the "aggressiveness" of Communist China, and so on. But surely the present political generation should not be made to pay for the failures of soured latter-day radicals.

Liberal realists are forever urging that we support government officials—especially if they speak in the idiom of liberalism. For they have access to privileged facts, and they normally do the best they can. Liberal officials do often deserve our understanding and even our compassion. If that is all that is meant by "support," I will not quarrel with the realist. But if he means that these officials also deserve our trust, then the radical liberal should be clear and definite in his reply: *no official ought to be trusted.* Not only do the contaminating epistemological factors described above operate on government officials, who tend more than most to be realists, but there are special reasons for mistrusting officials that have an absolutely decisive cumulative weight.

With the best liberal will in the world, government officials at the top of the totem pole are necessarily responsive to a system of political pressures that is bound to produce distortion of perception and judgment. A President is duty-bound to be responsive to the concerns expressed by members of the corporate elite, and of the John Birch Society as well as of the poor and of Negroes, if only because he must think of how most effectively to pursue a liberal legislative program. In addition, who can doubt that once a bad decision is made—especially bad decisions that cost vast sums of money and much American blood—it becomes psychologically almost impossible for the officials responsible to admit that they have erred. Kenneth Galbraith put the point that I am generalizing concretely when he wrote:

> Things have been going badly for the United States in South Vietnam for some time and to those of us who have been roughly in touch with the situation the reasons have seemed tolerably clear. The advocates of the wrong policy have been in charge and are deeply committed to their error. When things go wrong, they redouble their efforts, which, inevitably, makes things twice as bad.*

* *New York Herald Tribune*, Book Review Section, April 25, 1965.

Commitment to existing policy, right or wrong, is the highly probable destiny of public officials implicated in the formulation of that policy. To bring the French colonial wars in Indochina and Algeria to an end, there *had* to be a change of leadership.

In Vietnam, Robert McNamara has found his Edsel. At Ford, where profits are the final arbiter of managerial skill, he would undoubtedly have had the good sense to stop production by now. But for a government official, the criteria of success and failure are not so definite. Hence, even if he is a morally sensitive person—perhaps especially if he is a morally sensitive official—he will "redouble" his efforts if only because he cannot honestly face the prospect of conceding that his policy has squandered American lives. The true measure of President Kennedy's quite remarkable capacity for detached political judgment was that he could stop short of the final folly during the Bay of Pigs adventure—and could later admit that he had erred disastrously. But he was capable of the initial folly both there and in Vietnam; and few will deny that President Johnson, and most other liberal Presidents, have been more apt to display thin skin than cool intellectual judgment in such situations.

As for government officials farther down, consider their predicament. Not only are they constrained to advocate government policy by virtue of the formal definition of their offices, but there are other powerful psychological forces at work. For one thing, they share with key decision-makers the necessity of responding to the existing system of political pressures. More important, perhaps, is the fact that advancement in their careers depends on their learning how to play the bureaucratic game—and that means working diligently for a policy even when there is personal disagreement. But, at the same time, like any other human being, such an official needs to maintain his self-respect. If he is forced to advocate a policy of which he disapproves and if he is a person of any integrity, the psychic pain that results may be substantial. If the issue is momentous, and the official does not have the will or good sense to resign, then he is likely to make the psychological adjustments required for him truthfully to say that he accepts the offensive policy. And this will be so even if, on the basis of background and past record, it might seem inconceivable that he would. This is undoubtedly a good part of the story of Adlai Stevenson's final tragic months. A man who took as much pride in his record of honest public utterance, and who was as dedicated to the fundamental tasks of the United Nations as Stevenson, must have found it literally impossible either to escape his responsibilities or to defend policies with which he heartily disagreed. For, paradoxically, the Puritan in politics is heavily dependent on the approbation of peers to sustain his dedicated honesty. But how can he expect, or accept, the approbation of those he respects, unless he is capable of respecting himself? And how can he respect himself unless he accepts the policies he is bound to advocate in open council?

Given this impressive system of forces working to distort both the perception and judgment of all public officials, any ordinary citizen does well to view skeptically all who claim to know because they are specially rational or because they have access to privileged information—especially when the decisions involved are those most likely to whip up patriotic passion and the mindless support that results. Indeed, lacking other grounds, the patriotism of a free man in a free society would be sufficient to justify such skepticism.

A wise sovereign would have the intellect and strength of character to recognize this as the proper posture for the good citizen. He would realize not only that power tends to be used to manipulate others, but that it almost inevitably results in self-manipulation. This is why Rusk's advocacy of role-playing and President Johnson's puzzlement that any citizen would "feel toward his country in a way that is not consistent with the national interest" reveal a profoundly defective conception of the nature of democratic citizenship.

How does one protect himself against the ideological contaminations described? The short answer is, "not possible." But if complete freedom is out of the question, one can still progressively push back the boundaries of ideological bondage by acquiring the habit of reason and of Socratic self-examination; that is, by a lifelong educational experience that embodies precisely the features of the liberal conception of education yet to be described. For if one is going to be ideological in any event, the rational thing to do is to recognize it in order both to reduce its power of contamination and to exploit its possibilities—a much more sensible thing to do than to conduct spurious and self-deceiving polemics against ideological thinking.

And this brings me to the most basic objection one can make to the politics of pseudo-realism. Up to this point the assumption that politics is an amoral enterprise has not been challenged in detail. But the very fact that for most of us moral considerations are embodied in the ideological perspectives that shape even our judgments of fact implies that it is "unrealistic" to suppose that politics ever could be completely amoral. Still, the realist might insist that one should be as amoral as possible; that, so to speak, he should engage in strenuous moral exercise on Sunday morning, but during political hours he should engage in strenuous amoral exercise.

The first thing that is wrong with this counsel is that it is schizophrenic, resulting in a destructive lack of authenticity. Even if it were possible, it would be painfully inconvenient. A person cannot be moral in one sphere and amoral in another without becoming self-alienated. For this reason alone, the suggestion is profoundly illiberal in spirit and application. It destroys the possibility of the ideal that lies at the heart of liberalism: self-development.

Beyond this consideration, the idea that moral principles are irrelevant to the assessment of the means to desirable ends is morally vicious. It is moral Stalinism—the view that considerations of justice are irrelevant to the means adopted.

There may be times when the ends pursued are of such overwhelming importance that considerations of justice may legitimately be overridden—for example, a situation in which national survival is literally at stake. But even in such a case, the principles of justice are relevant, and must *be overridden*. In most ordinary political contexts, the desirable aim does not have such supervening importance. For example, there are those who do not hesitate to rally Negroes to a civil rights cause by manipulating them, "for their own good," with lies and racial rhetoric. In so doing, the manipulator simply subjects to indignity those he professes to rescue from indignity. For, more than anything else, the respect due others requires respect for powers of mind and spirit.

In the making of foreign policy, the idea that morality is irrelevant is more complex because it has a certain Hobbesian plausibility. The Hobbesian view is that as politically sovereign societies are not governed by laws, they exist in "a state of nature" that precludes morality because it is psychologically impossible for states to act morally. There are, as a friend once put it, few "wanderers among nations." Therefore, the ultimate test of the propriety of policy is its contribution to national interest.

The argument is unsound, however, for two reasons. First, the conception of "national interest" is a blank check upon which one inscribes any interest, including moral interests, that are important. Therefore, foreign policy is going to be controlled by ideological considerations in any event. But second, even granting that wanderers among nations are not plentiful, they do occur—and the aim of liberal policy should be to increase their number. Here, if anywhere, James' claim that what is possible is a function of what is believed to be possible has decisive application.

Realism and Democracy

The foregoing analysis makes it easy to understand why the liberal realist tends to favor an exclusively countervailing conception of democracy. He aims to get things done—to be effective. He wants the facts about how one gets things done. The facts confirm what the emphasis on effectiveness suggests—that gaining and managing power is the central problem of political life. The amoral character of the realist's judgment reinforces what exclusive preoccupation with power encourages—a dulling of one's concern about the quality of the process by which power is secured and managed.

The liberal realist favors political democracy over all competing systems for three reasons: it is the process which most efficaciously secures social stability, the general welfare, and human rights. (Note: liberal realists who are deeply concerned about securing human rights as a policy objective are often too quick to violate them in the process if that is what effective action requires.)

The emphases on stability and general welfare are interdependent. Stability is achieved through a process by which the maximum number of human preferences are satisfied. But through satisfaction of preferences general welfare is cumulatively secured. It is no accident, therefore, that the most influential theorists of the countervailing power conception of democracy in recent years have been economists—particularly Joseph Schumpeter. For the countervailing conception of democracy is modeled on the economists' marketplace. It is a process whereby the consumer (the voter) shops around for the commodities (candidates and policies) that best satisfy his preferences (interests). By giving his business to one firm (political party) rather than to its competitors, he enables that firm better to gain profit (office, patronage, status) and power. The competing firms try to induce consumers to stop buying the competitor's products, and to buy their own. This they may do by offering different products which they claim to be of higher quality, by inventing new products (new policies), or by lowering the price they charge for the same products (lowering taxes). This competitive process is very practical; very realistic; very amoral. But, as in any market economy, there are many competitive frictions. These exact a long-term moral and aesthetic cost which is unanticipated and enormous. Most important, the process is intrinsically destructive of rights and of the opportunities to develop the capacities for good citizenship in the most liberal sense of that expression.

The "realism" of the market is buttressed by a "realistic" assessment of human nature. The countervailing power theorist may, like Schumpeter, claim that it is the best way to counteract man's irrational tendencies. Or, like Reinhold Niebuhr, he may proclaim that man is born in sin, and that the countervailing power process is the surest antidote to original depravity.

All the criticisms of pseudo-realism already developed apply to exclusive reliance on a democracy of countervailing power. Preoccupation with power is ideologically influenced. The democratic process prescribed is immoral because it squanders human rights and potentialities. It is self-defeating because it undermines the very conditions of deliberative citizenship. It is unrealistic because it is the worst possible way to ensure that political leadership will have the "managerial skills" necessary to function most effectively in pursuit of liberal aims. But basically, its pessimistic cast is self-fulfilling. By diminishing liberalism's political reach, it forfeits many liberal aims that are within liberalism's grasp. In the end, Freud's principle fully applies to those who place exclusive reliance on the countervailing power conception. Each such individual is governed by deep-rooted internal prejudices into whose hands his practicality unwittingly plays.

4

THE
POLITICS
OF
SELF-
INDULGENCE

Arthur Schlesinger, Jr., attributes the Bay of Pigs disaster partly to the fact that President Kennedy's liberal advisors were trying desperately to prove that they were really tough guys, and not soft-headed idealists.* What does an authentic liberal do when liberalism is perverted in this way by powerful men who are regarded as liberals? What does he do once he fully acknowledges the enormous gap between the promises of American rhetoric and the reality of American society? What does he do when it becomes obvious that many who talk in the idiom of "political effectiveness" are really trying to disguise self-serving pursuit of personal ambition? What does he do in order to avoid absorption by the agencies of "the Establishment" that seem to know how to defer to the

* *A Thousand Days*, Boston, Houghton Mifflin, 1965, p. 256.

existing structures of power better than to anything else? One thing he may do is purchase immunity from the sickness of pseudo-realism by forgoing any prospect of effective political action. He can repudiate the system that breeds and sustains the evils he despises. Unfortunately, in rejecting the system he also forfeits access to institutional resources which he must control if liberal ideals are to be effectively pursued. Thus, he sacrifices the prospects of political success for the sake of his soul. He practices the politics of self-indulgence.

The Search for Authenticity

When one prominent liberal, sickened by the Administration's Vietnam policy, decided to resign from the Democratic party, he justified himself in the following terms:

> The major issue in most of the criticisms of my letter to the President has been whether leaving the Democratic party makes political sense.
>
> Of course it does not. Anyone wanting to exert maximum political leverage would stay in the party, organize dissenting precinct leaders and district leaders, and see that their protest appeared in newspaper columns and advertisements and, if possible, on the desk of the President himself. This is the kind of politics to which the President responds. *If I were of a different temperament I would have done just that.* [My emphasis.]*

What interests me here is not the action itself: in balance, it may have been the right thing to do. What interests me is this liberal's implicit assumption that the indulgence of his peculiar temperament is a justification in itself. Others go a bit farther. They proclaim that their predominant concern is to achieve "personal authenticity." They also condemn as "finks" liberals who refuse to participate in their projects of

* W. H. Ferry, "The Brutalization of Violence," *Liberation*, October 1965.

protest when those projects seem ineffective or counter-productive. But—and this is my central point—between "finkdom" and violent revolution there may be only the career of noisy impotence, despair, and eventual absorption by the hated "establishment."

Many of those who practice the politics of self-indulgence are young men and women who join "the Movement" and thereby become members of the "New Left." Not all of those who act self-indulgently are to be found in the Movement; nor do all members of that movement practice the politics of self-indulgence. I am abstracting a recognizable tendency that expresses itself to a significant extent in the political activity of many American liberals. They may not call themselves "liberals," nor even think of themselves as liberals. But they are committed to liberal ideals as I have described them; and that is what counts. In a brilliant essay, Irving Howe described those who practice the politics of self-indulgence as making "of their radicalism not a politics of common action, which would require the inclusion of saints, sinners, and ordinary folk, but rather a gesture of moral rectitude."* Much of what I have to say recapitulates Howe's argument; but it is important to view this form of political life from the perspective of radical-liberalism.

Those who practice the politics of self-indulgence are the moral victims of the dialectic of disorder. Many are Negroes whose souls are sickened by the sand-bagging moderation that passes for responsible citizenship. Many come from middle-class backgrounds where they have been daily witnesses to the corrupting insincerity of the lives led by their parents. Most have been subjected to what passes for education in our multiversities. All are fed up with the self-deception and hypocrisy of those who practice pseudo-realism.

They are properly suspicious of people who talk in the idiom of effectiveness—for the stress on effectiveness is too

---

* "New Styles in Leftism," *Dissent*, Summer 1965.

often a cover for the comforts of quiescence and the preoccupation with a pursuit of successful careers. They refuse to succumb to red-baiting, and are rightly contemptuous of those who try to dismiss them by labeling them "Stalinoid."

They despise Stalinism and all its works. Which is, indeed, why they react with moral outrage to the double standard of those liberal realists who advocate the defense of "freedom" by means that are often not very different from those Stalin employed in Russia. (Yet they, too, often slip into Stalinist grooves when they proclaim their admiration for revolutionary excesses on the grounds that revolution does not, after all, occur "in a velvet box"—a point developed subsequently.)

They are appalled by the failures and distortions of democracy in this country. They are deeply committed to the proposition that those who are vitally affected by large decisions have a right to participate in making those decisions in ways more meaningful than an occasional vote. And so they advocate a democracy of participation, hearkening back to the Jeffersonian tradition of direct participation that has existed since the birth of the Republic as an unrealized part of the rhetoric of Americanism, while the Madisonian tradition of coalition politics has triumphed. So, also, they move into the ghettoes, the slums, and the rural areas of the South, to work directly with those who have been bypassed by American affluence. Their aspiration is to induce those with whom they work to take firmer control of their own destinies so that the tides of modernity will no longer pass over or engulf them.

Oppressed by the pervasive hypocrisy of American society; smothered by the institutional acquisitiveness of established interests; tyrannized by the benevolent paternalism of academic administrators; dirtied by the philistinism and ugliness of the prevailing American culture (how much better to be dirty on the outside and clean on the inside, than the reverse); stultified by the mindlessness of the realists who purvey what passes for social wisdom; oppressed by the manipulativeness of those who pursue the Great Society; they are propelled into a desperate pursuit of authenticity that requires, for the younger radicals, generational mistrust. The worst cut of all is that private virtue, an exemplary life of absolute middle-class integrity, is not only consistent with, but often the very vehicle of, public vice.

Their search takes them out of the mainstream and into the murkier tributaries of American life. Hence, many try to find their freedom in practices that shock conventional morality; in sexual abandon, filthy speech, LSD and marijuana clubs, beards and dirt; but also in song, poetry, and art; in the theatre of the absurd, as if its absurdity could mitigate the absurdity of their own lives; but, more than anything else, in political action and protest. For if there are dragons to be slain, one has to go where the action is. This, at least, is what they have learned since the era of Salinger. Those liberals who currently use the "Beatniks" and the "Vietniks" as whipping posts should remember that those they abuse are not just talking freedom; they are trying to live freely.

The civil rights struggle provided a remarkable opportunity to combine the search for authenticity with effective acts of protest. For a variety of reasons, direct action has proved to be an immensely successful means of forcing the pace and nature of civil rights reform. The relative clarity of the moral issues, the large proportion of the population directly involved, the vulnerability of local officials, the exclusion of Southern Negroes from even a formal role in the governing processes, the unconstitutionality of many state and local statutes, the extent to which the civil rights movement has been able to neutralize the Communist issue—all these factors have combined to enable those most committed to less conventional forms of political action to achieve significant success. Unfortunately, the same set of favorable circumstances that has made it possible to be both "authentic" and effective in the fight for civil rights does not occur in every sphere in which the struggle for social justice is carried on—and is, perhaps, disappearing fast even in civil rights. The casual ways in which civil rights tactics have been employed in opposing American foreign policies have, in balance, especially retarded the effort to force liberal change—a point I will develop in more detail later.

The Trap of Inauthenticity

Although the strength of their feelings, the legitimacy of their moral concerns, and their desire to do something effective should lead them to vigorous intervention in the normal political process, many members of "the Movement" have grown impatient with the calculations and compromises that effective participation in that process imposes. They are, as I have said, too often concerned more with the state of their souls than with the preferences and welfare of those they aim to help. They are too often unwilling to act in ways they regard as inauthentic for the sake of a greater prospect of definite results.

Their acts are self-indulgent, first because even if loss of authenticity were the inevitable result of the calculation and compromise that effective action requires, damage to one's self ought to be balanced against the resulting sacrifices imposed on others. For the middle-class children of middle-class parents have somewhere else to go if they fail. But where do the oppressed of Vietnam or the inhabitants of Tent City in Lowndes County, Alabama, have to go? Too often the well-educated scions of prosperous families are prepared to fight for human rights to the last indigent before beating their perilous way back to lucrative professional careers.

Second, the politics described is self-indulgent because the definition of authenticity endorsed is spurious. The notion that authenticity requires that one forgo calculation and compromise is perverse. I have many reasons for claiming that this is so.

First, many of those who justify their actions on grounds of personal authenticity mask their ineffectiveness, even from themselves, by adopting Leninist rhetoric without participating in Leninist revolutionary aims—and I mean *violent* revolution. They subject the system they repudiate to an abusive hammer attack that inspires the converted and alienates everyone else. Hence, like those liberals they so bitterly criticize, members of the Movement create a gap between their own rhetoric and their social reality. To the extent that this is so, they are at least as insincere as those they condemn. Worse—they are ineffectual.

Given this basic insincerity, they could close the gap by becoming revolutionary in fact as well as in word. But they won't. They are too middle-class in sentiment and aspiration. They have too much bourgeois ideology in their system. Their very disaffection is proof of the fact—for it is a disaffection rooted in their serious acceptance of liberal ideals. Nor is their commitment to bourgeois values a fault. For the test of the validity of any value is not its social origin. If certain bourgeois values are also the values of a civilized humanism, then let us make the most of them. Failure to make this discrimination is an intellectual fault.

Moreover, they know very well that revolution would not only fail, but the attempt would cause incalculably more harm than good. For all its defects, American society is progressive in the perspective of history. Emmanuel Geltman and Stanley Plastrik put the point precisely:

Legislation must be implemented by enforcement and education. Meanwhile we must distinguish between what we have lost and what we have won, and that means learning to recognize what we have won. Inadequate as much of the legislation seems, our perception of its inadequacy rests upon the advances which it embodies. It is downright silly to maintain that nothing has been achieved. Who will tell that to an auto worker who remembers the Ford plant thirty years ago? Or Mrs. Parks?*

It is not only what has been won that counts. What has been won is due to the genius with which America's powerful and privileged elites have, since the Civil War, been able to buy off discontent through peripheral remedy of grievances. Yet enough peripheral movement equals substantial social change. This is but the reflection in institutional development of coalition politics at work. The fact that Americans over-whelmingly prefer what they have, with all its defects, to what revolution would bring is not only the curse but the triumph of the American system so ingeniously designed by James Madison and his cohorts more than two centuries ago. Members of the Movement may not be willing to say it. But that does not matter. The fact is, *they know it*. And so they insincerely draw back from their rhetoric without yet being able to accept their reality.

But there is an area in which they can match deed to rhetoric—in foreign policy. For it is not they who must make the revolution in Cuba, South Africa, or Vietnam. And so they can and do proclaim the ideals of liberal humanism and at the same time proclaim, as did one SDS leader, that "revolutions do not take place in velvet boxes." In this way they try to answer those liberal critics who refuse to condone the terror and the tyranny that oppressed people or the elites who lead them perpetrate in trying to rid themselves of their chains. Or they persuasively define the word "terror" and proclaim that the terror committed is all our own. But this is only to abuse both mind and sensibility. For they resort to non sequitur in a demagogic effort to win more support for a cause than the cause morally deserves.

The inauthenticity of members of "the Movement" is evidenced in still another way. They rely for support on the

* "The Politics of Coalition," in Irving Howe, ed., *The Radical Papers*, New York, Doubleday, 1966, p. 375.

"finks" they abuse. And they usually get the support that saves them from their folly. But when that support is not enough to prevent penalty, they are inappropriately shocked and dismayed—"inappropriately," because if they believed what they say when they abuse the "finks," they should find support astonishing, and its failure only to be expected. When they succeed in gaining effective support from liberal "finks," they like to think that it is the result of clever manipulations. It is inconceivable to them that those who defend their rights act out of genuine moral commitment rather than bad conscience. (At that, even bad conscience reflects commitment—if less than the "pure" motivation to which many members of the Movement aspire.)

Which brings me to still another form of inauthenticity. The very persons who proclaim their absolute and undying commitment to a nonmanipulative democracy of participation too often employ the opportunities such a system affords in manipulative and undemocratic ways. Charismatic leaders declare charisma nonexistent—but, all the same, use it to gain their ends. Like the mentors they despise, they profess what they do not practice. Here again, the defect is one of intellect—in two respects. They confuse mere involvement with a democracy of participation by means of which the growth of powers of mind and spirit are encouraged. And they lack the power to discriminate when they fall short in their own conduct of their own ideal aspiration.

Finally, it must be said that some who justify their predilection for dramatic protest in terms of authenticity are really masking from themselves their unwillingness to commit themselves to sustained political involvement. A dramatic flare-up involves a major commitment for a limited period. Thus conscience can be appeased at little cost in time and effort. This is both spiritually uplifting and comfortable if one has ambitions that pull in other directions.

But most of those who practice the politics of self-indulgence are at the other extreme. They have a capacity for sustained political involvement that does not normally need to be reinforced by the more conventional political rewards—power and prestige, office and income. This energy for work is in rather scarce supply in this country. When it occurs, it is to be valued—no matter how it happens to be packaged. For the indispensable condition of achievement is, under any and all conditions, the willingness to work.

Moreover, it is impossible to deny that those who are willing to give unstintingly also make other contributions. They are often the initiators of action. They have a political rhetoric of their own which generates new aspirations, new frustrations, new and creative forms of political movement and public policy. From their ranks emerge the poets, and the martyrs of change. Their very passion for authenticity, however defectively expressed in specific situations, is a model and an inspiration.

But to be an inspiration is one thing; to be effective in the long run, quite another. For that kind of success, something more substantial than moral passion, romantic exuberance, and unstinting effort is required. What is needed is a new breed of indefatigable radicals, passionately moral, yes—but also coldly calculating and unfailingly energetic in pursuit of liberal goals. As John Fisher has recently put it: "What this country needs is radicals who will stay that way—regardless of the creeping years, the inevitable blunders, defeats, and combat fatigue."* Will the young men and women of "the Movement" pass that test? Not unless they come to realize that they are destined to despair—and that that despair will turn to quiescence or be converted into Madison Avenue cynicism and ambition—unless they acquire disciplines of reason in the same measure that they already possess moral concern.

* *Harper's Magazine*, March 1966, p. 28.

5 THE ALTERNATIVE: DEMOCRACY AND THE POLITICS OF RADICAL PRESSURE

Radical-liberals have two fundamental tasks: to translate their theoretical principles and aims into concrete programs, and to develop a strategic concept that has as many of the strengths and as few of the weaknesses of the two deranged political styles as possible. In this section I undertake to define the second of these tasks.

It is not enough to be concerned only with the effectiveness of a strategy. A political process is not just a means of implementing political programs. The process itself has an impact on participants that may speed or retard achievement of the values liberals cherish. The central claim of John Dewey's philosophy was that the democratic process could enrich the lives of men not only by what it does for them but by what it does to them. In the following passage from his book, *The Public and Its Problems*, Dewey expresses the point with prophetic eloquence:

We have but touched lightly and in passing upon the conditions which must be fulfilled if the Great Society is to become a Great Community; a society in which the ever-expanding and intricately ramifying consequences of associated activities shall be known in the full sense of that word, so that an organized, articulate Public comes into being. The highest and most difficult kind of inquiry and a subtle, delicate, vivid, and responsive art of communication must take possession of the physical machinery of transmission and circulation and breathe life into it. When the machine age has thus perfected its machinery it will be a means of life and not its despotic master. Democracy will come into its own, for democracy is a name for a life of free and enriching communion. It had its seer in Walt Whitman. It will have its consummation when free social inquiry is indissolubly wedded to the art of full and moving communication.*

The point crystallized by Dewey's remarks is that an adequate conception of liberal strategy must be based on an adequate conception of liberal democracy. Effective pursuit of legislative programs is normally purchased at a price higher than liberals need to pay if the political processes adopted do little to improve in mind and spirit those who participate and those who are affected; if the accepted conception of democracy does not promote the fullest possible range of liberal values.

The Functions of Democracy

The set of values that democracy ought to promote has been an issue on which many of the preceding arguments have turned. I want now to tie together the threads of those discussions; and, by describing six functions democracy ought to serve, to provide a theoretical solvent for the two contrasting conceptions of democracy—participatory and countervailing power democracy—that figure so importantly in current debate among liberals.

* *The Public and Its Problems*, p. 184.

i. Democracy should reinforce the stabilizing institutions of a society. There are times in the life of a society when the imperatives of order must be rejected in favor of violent revolution. But normally democracy functions as a means of expressing grievances and interests in ways that reduce the general level of discontent, and thereby diminish pressures for redress of grievance through the use of force. This is the first and minimal goal of democratic organization—but, for that very reason, the least distinctive of its functions. The concern for stability is a social virtue only to the extent that it facilitates definite and substantial progress toward liberal goals; not when it is a thinly disguised excuse for sand-bagging realistic pursuit of those ends.

ii. One of these goals is the protection of rights. A democratic system should be organized so that freedoms essential to equal development of human potentialities are securely protected. No other tradition has been as steady and relentless in its *theoretical* repudiation of tyrannical power. But, for that very reason, the gap between liberal theory and liberal practice is a special disaster.

iii. Generally the maintenance of order and the protection of rights require that human preferences be satisfied. In this way a sufficient number of grievances are eliminated before distress reaches dangerous proportions. The satisfaction of existing human preferences does not, however, always promote the conditions of personal self-development. For men do not always know what is best for them. Yet, if vulgar democrats mistakenly suppose that the voice of the people is the voice of God, the mistake that theorists of aristocracy or meritocracy make is in supposing that anyone else can be given power undemocratically because he is presumed to know better. First, it is notoriously difficult to establish criteria for such knowledge. Second, who can better guarantee that a leader who has the knowledge will use it wisely except the people who must suffer or enjoy the consequences of his social policies? But subjection of leadership to the will of the people implies that satisfaction of existing preferences will generally be pursued. For these reasons, the promotion of general welfare through satisfaction of existing preferences is, with all its dangers, an essential goal of liberalism—and an important function of democracy.

iv. One of the special rights liberals cherish is the freedom of persons to participate in the making of those social policies that vitally affect their destinies. In this respect there is not even a theoretical alternative to democratic process. The satisfaction of this function should be an intrinsic virtue of that process.

v. Intimately related to the right of participation is the liberal concern that the virtues of responsible citizenship be developed in the largest possible number of people. This primarily means that the citizen's respect for the traditions of reason and for his own capacities should be encouraged. Democracy is defective to the extent that it is not constituted in processes that serve this function. If, as Dewey claimed, a by-product is "enriching communion," all the better.

vi. Wise political leadership is an essential condition of right policy in any and all conditions. The central mistake of antidemocratic theorists is not their stress on the importance of leadership but their belief that effective leadership requires dictatorial or total power. The liberal insists that good leadership is at least as much a matter of being able to influence the course of events through reasoned persuasion as it is the shaping of destinies by manipulating people and power. Effective leadership depends at least as much on the kind of sensitivity to human needs and preferences produced by the processes of direct and mutually respectful involvement with those led as it does upon technical expertise.

Against the background of this catalogue of the functions of democracy, the conflict, though not the tension, between the theorists of a countervailing, or coalition, conception of democracy, and the theorists of a democracy of participation, disappears. For *both* are essential, but in different functional respects. This is what I now aim to show.

Two Conceptions of Democracy

James Madison was the great theorist of a democracy of countervailing coalitions. Never in history has an emerging institutional process conformed as closely to design as the American political process has to the system he envisioned, especially in his *Federalist Paper No. 10.* Jean-Jacques Rousseau, though less prophetic, holds a similar place of pride among theorists of participatory democracy.

In his book, *The Social Contract,* Rousseau held that only in a small-scale democracy of participation can both justice and rational public policy be secured. In particular, he believed that once a society adopts a representative system of government, one may "give over the state for lost." Madison argued that Rousseau's form of "pure democracy" will inevitably degenerate into anarchy and tyranny; that only a system of countervailing coalitions buttressed by what he called "auxiliary precautions" can protect individual rights, especially property rights, and maintain social stability.

In the argument that follows I try to show, by means of a dialectical modification of both the Madisonian and Rousseauan positions, how one can arrive at a view that satisfies the six functional requirements stated previously; a conception of democracy that promotes the fullest range of liberal values by encouraging creative tension between the processes the two men advocated.

A Madisonian might initially insist that the Rousseauan is a romantic, and somewhat reactionary, visionary. He might claim that the possibility of small-scale democracies of participation ended when industrialization made city-states the size of Athens and Geneva impossible. The Rousseauan, he might claim, talks in the idiom of the radical, but in fact fights modernity. The only thing direct democracy will ever bring about is anarchy and consequent tyranny. It is not, he might continue, even necessary to retell Thucydides' story. Consider what happened to the industrial Soviets established during the early years of the Bolshevik Revolution. It didn't take Lenin very long to realize that, contrary to what Marx prophesied and what Lenin himself hoped for, this experiment in participatory democracy was a disaster. He might claim that Lenin's misbegotten experiment paved the way for Stalinist tyranny. "Be realistic," he might urge. "Work within the framework of coalition politics that has proved, not perfect, but the best political process human beings have been able to devise."

The Rousseauan could reasonably admit that *The Social Contract* cannot be applied as it was written. Too much has happened since the middle of the eighteenth century. But he might go on to deny that Rousseau's central assumptions, suitably applied to modern industrial conditions, are irrelevant or unimportant. Rousseau, it is true, was wrong to claim that once representative institutions are permitted, the state is lost. Nevertheless, unless a system of coalition politics is invigorated by participatory institutions, important values are needlessly forfeited, the prospect of urgently needed radical reform is destroyed and, equally important, the prospect of improving the quality of the processes of coalition politics is severely limited.

To this the Madisonian might reply that the only system that can insure stable social conditions, provide adequate protection against tyrannical abuse of human rights, and maximize social welfare is a politics of countervailing power. By dispersing power through a nation vast in population and geographic extent, and by guaranteeing to a sufficiently large portion of that population the vote, the ruling coalitions that emerge are rendered inherently unstable. Frequent elections give the "outs" an opportunity to attract, by means of new programs, the factions peripheral to the ruling coalition. Auxiliary protections like the Supreme Court and the federal system itself provide additional brakes on tyrannical abuse of power. Each faction will associate itself with others for limited purposes of mutual benefit. When the particular purposes of any of these factions are achieved, they will go fishing in different political waters. Except for the Civil War, which was due to the rigidities created by the "peculiar institution" of slavery and the unnatural economic homogeneity of different regions of the country, the system has worked well as a means of maintaining stability, and tolerably well as a barrier to violation of human rights.

The Rousseauan could retort that the Madisonian has missed his point. He no longer denies the strengths imputed to the Madisonian system; but the Madisonian should not, in turn, overlook the intrinsic value as well as the necessary corrective supplied by participatory democracy. Most Madisonians, being economically well off and high in status, rarely calculate the human price that is paid for the kind of stability and progress they cherish. The total product may be increasing, but it is not being distributed equally. General welfare is not equal welfare. The fact that almost a third of the people of the United States hardly participate in our vaunted affluence is not a historical accident, but is due to the system's chronic defects. Political leadership is almost all drawn from the prosperous classes. Madison thought that wealthy people would be more likely than others to be men of light and learning. But his assumption has proved to be a piece of class prejudice. Some rights are, from the Madisonian point of view, more equal than others—particularly property rights. And this is not acceptable to a radical-liberal. Moreover, consider the gratingly slow processes by which grievances are remedied in a Madisonian system. This can be mitigated by more intimate decision-making structures. Even granting that the system of countervailing coalitions is, in balance, an engine for progress—one must consider the frictional factors that grind living people down. The Madisonian is too inclined to tolerate almost any human price for stability and protection of property rights—provided it is "only" those most oppressed by the system who are required to pay that price. The high casualty rates among Negroes in our "defense of freedom" in Vietnam is just the latest and most dramatic example of what this means in human terms. But worst of all is the way in which the Madisonian system causes policy to gravitate toward a political consensus based on accidental configurations of factional interests rather than on reason and morality.

The man in the White House says, "Come let us reason together." But radical-liberals know that too often he really means, "Come, let me manipulate you." Increasingly, powerful leaders work their will by relying on the manipulative arts and the mindlessness of citizens and legislators. A democracy of participation would be one way, perhaps the most important, in which a broader spectrum of the population can be educated in the virtues of responsible citizenship, and thus inoculated against the unreason of the manipulators. At the same time, it will make more likely the emergence of political leadership from a stratum of the population who presently depend too often upon the patricians of American politics to fight their political battles. But beyond both these advantages, ordinary people simply have the right to participate more fully in the policy decisions that vitally affect their lives.

The Madisonian might shift his ground a bit, and accuse the Rousseauan of endorsing what Bayard Rustin has called a "no-win tendency." In his article "From Protest to Politics?"* Rustin wrote:

> My quarrel with the "no-win" tendency in the civil rights movement [Rustin would have the same quarrel with the

* Reprinted in Irving Howe, ed., *The Radical Papers*, New York, Doubleday, 1966, p. 342.

"no-win" tendencies on the "New Left" generally] parallels my quarrel with the moderates outside the movement. As the latter lack the vision or will for fundamental change, the former lack a realistic strategy for achieving it. For such a strategy they substitute militancy. But militancy is a matter of posture and volume, not of effect.

His conclusion is based on recognition that "the Negro today finds himself stymied by obstacles of far greater magnitude than the legal barriers he was attacking before: automation, urban decay, de facto school segregation." He argues that these defects are much more deeply rooted in our socioeconomic order than the legal props to segregation. They are the result of a total societal failure to meet not just the needs of Negroes but human needs generally.

Now how do you cope effectively with these larger problems, except by finding allies among others who either oppose the system or, because they are injured by it, are potential opponents? A coalition of Negroes, liberals, students, laborers, migrant farmers, Mexicans, poor "white trash," Puerto Ricans, and anyone else who does not or should not like the way things are, organized in mutually advantageous ways, stands some prospect of success. In other words Rustin advocates that the political resources of the existing Madisonian system be used as effectively as possible. Though it may be personally satisfying to indulge one's preference for acts of direct political involvement—whether building structures of communal participation or protest—to do this to the exclusion of participation in coalition politics will be self-defeating in the long run.

Unless one is self-deceived by revolutionary rhetoric, it is impossible to deny the cogency of Rustin's argument. The Rousseauan may admit as much; yet he may also deny any suggestion that Rustin's position either precludes or makes unimportant efforts to create participatory institutions. (Nor does Rustin suppose otherwise.)

For, though interested in a "win" policy as much as

Rustin, the Rousseauan would want to make sure that our definition of what it is to "win" is not restricted to the implementation of a legislative program. There are things that the very process of *trying to win* can do to people. If they participate in an increasingly deliberative process, they can develop their powers of mind and spirit.* And, as suggested before, unless such a process is encouraged, the prospects of winning even legislative reform are impaired.

A citizenry involved is more likely to become interested and politically motivated than persons who are encouraged only to cast a biennial vote. By being thrown into situations in which they must think not just about the relative merits of candidates but about the policies themselves, they are more likely to acquire the knowledge, the sense of relevance, and the skills of the mind to persist more resolutely and more thoughtfully in the fight for programs that will be more than a welfare-tinted anodyne for distress caused by massive need. And they will be more likely to produce a leadership from their own ranks that cannot be bought off.

Rustin's argument is correct as far as it goes—but it doesn't go far enough. Coalition politics can be effective without being as effective as possible.

At this point the Madisonian should be prepared to concede a great deal to the Rousseauan. He would, if he is honest and liberal, have to concede that for many Americans things have worked out badly. He would also have to admit that he was wrong in stressing stability and the protection of rights, especially property rights, to the exclusion of so much else. But he may still be distressed by the Rousseauan's tendency to think of the countervailing form of coalition politics solely in terms of effectiveness, reserving all

---

* To some extent this is what concerns the young militants of SNCC. Acutely aware that Negroes of the black belt have been deprived of self-confidence and self-esteem by their virtual bondage, SNCC views participation as an important remedy. They regard coalition politics as a means of perpetuating spiritual entrapment. Cf. Chapter 6 for a fuller discussion of this claim.

the moral virtues for participatory democracy. Even from the Rousseauan's point of view, the system of coalition politics has some advantages that go beyond the question of mere effectiveness.

For one thing, it provides a larger framework of forces and interests that inhibits the provincialism and factionalism that so often contaminate deliberations within more intimately organized political structures.

For another, whatever is achieved through the politics of countervailing power promotes the values that result from participatory democracy by strengthening the motive to participate. Romantic exuberance is fine, but unless it is sustained by occasional success at the more general policy levels, enthusiasm will soon evaporate. Morale and motive cannot be sustained by the intensity of initial commitment alone.

Moreover, the system of countervailing powers does provide that degree of protection from interference by corporate powers, public and private, that is essential to the functioning of participatory institutions. And it also creates that floor of material benefits that the maligned welfare state affords; and without which a democracy of participation will not last for very long. One can, for example, deplore the inadequacies of the Poverty Program, but it is indirectly subsidizing a lot of the activity that the Rousseauan favors. And, even if this were not so, persons who face the prospect of actual starvation will have neither the time nor the inclination to engage in "participatory deliberations."

Finally, no matter how much the conservative preoccupation with stability and order is impugned, in a less ideological moment the Rousseauan will have to admit that a degree of stability and order are conditions without which the growth of a deliberative democracy of participation would be an impossibility.

But it is important to be clear that stability and order are to be understood in a way that permits political conflict, dissent, protest, and radical change. They are, by implication, to be understood in a way that makes them compatible with forms of political action that conservatives, quick on the verbal draw, are inclined to regard as "disorderly processes." Above all, the stabilizing processes of a society should not only permit but actively encourage reasoned scrutiny and criticism of its most sacred institutions and beliefs. An unexamined society may be worth living in; but the constraints it imposes are hardly worthy of those who proclaim that they are free men in a free society. And the protection of "sacred institutions and beliefs" too often becomes a flimsy self-serving mask for the protection of existing structures of power and prerogative.

At this point the fundamental opposition between the two positions breaks down. The Madisonian and the Rousseauan may arrive at a limited agreement. The latter claims that coalition politics without participatory democracy tends to be irresponsible, manipulative, and class dominated. The former claims that participatory democracy without coalition politics tends to be provincial, factional, and lacking in necessary political and material props—i.e., stability, welfare, and a framework of protected rights. They are both right. In the final analysis, the two institutional processes are essential to one another because in important respects they complement and reinforce one another. This is so even though in other respects there is, and always must be, unresolved tension between them.

The Prerequisites of Madisonian Democracy

The general case for participatory institutions is strengthened by relating the point about the mutual interdependence of the two processes to an old liberal perplexity. Just what attitude should a liberal democrat take toward underdeveloped societies that do not permit full freedom of political opposition?

Previously I observed that liberal theorists have generally acknowledged that there exist cultural and industrial prerequisites for a formal democracy of countervailing power. But liberal theories of democracy have rarely proposed definite criteria on the basis of which one could assess the extent to which democratization of these societies had been achieved, nor liberal guidelines for determining how to rub out deficiencies that impede progress toward political democracy. By and large, liberals have tended to echo the conventional response—that education, industrialization, rule of law, and a few, precariously established, formal freedoms are sufficient evidence of adequate democratization of the society.

These tests tend to be strengthened or relaxed depending on whether one is militantly anti-Communist or militantly pro-revolutionary. The anti-Communist liberal will apply the democracy test more stringently to "pro-Communist" or revolutionary societies, less stringently to anti-Communist societies. Many radicals, on the other hand, tend to suppose that for societies in the throes of revolutionary ferment industrialization alone will do. Industrialization cannot, after all, take place in a velvet box any more than violent revolution itself. So bloody suppression, not only of organized political opposition, but of speech, press, and other "bourgeois" rights is not always rejected as completely as it should be. For example, I have never been able to understand why someone cannot view Castroism both as progressive in certain industrial and social respects, and as tyrannical and reactionary to the extent that the Castro régime has dismantled the traditional structures of rule of law—especially as the despised legal institutions seemed to have functioned well enough to have enabled Castro himself to escape imprisonment during his earliest period of rebelliousness.

The point is that the conventional criteria are not very satisfactory because they do not enable us to make fine enough discriminations. By the conventional tests alone Russia, for example, would have to be said to be moving more rapidly toward democracy than is Pakistan or Egypt. Perhaps this is so; but there is another property of the last two systems that Russia lacks.

Both Pakistan and Egypt have tried to incorporate an element of participatory democracy into their respective social systems. Pakistan has done so roughly on the model of India's experiments in village democracy; Egypt, more or less, on the model of Yugoslavia's experiments with workers' councils. If what I have argued is sound, the development of these growing points for democracy outside the conventional framework of more or less autocratic power should both augur well for the future of political democracy in these countries and, incidentally, yield an important new criterion by which to assess underdeveloped nations that are not democracies in the sense of permitting organized political opposition at all levels of power. Many countries seem, in fact, to be adopting such experiments in one form or another.

Indeed, just to pursue this line of thinking to its domestic conclusion, perhaps what is good for India and Pakistan, Egypt and Yugoslavia, is good for Mississippi, Alabama, and even, pardon the unrealistic thought, for New York City.

The Iron Law of Oligarchy

The Madisonian may not yet be able to shake the conviction that there is something deeply unrealistic about a democracy of participation. There seems to be some overriding obstacle to this form of democracy, something rooted deeply in the very nature of man and of his institutions—an iron law of organization that decrees that any social movement will either be transformed into organization, or wither and die. And, as Michels and the other elite theorists argued, there seems further to be an iron law of oligarchy which decrees that, in any organization, pure democracy will inevitably be supplanted by oligarchy. Indeed, some sociologists believe the institutional and psychological forces that make for personal irresponsibility to be so powerful, that they have come to regard widespread apathy as a virtue of any social system.

The problems raised by these heroic criticisms will not here be discussed in the sociological and psychological detail required. But, in line with the earlier criticism of the politics of pseudo-realism, this much must be said: After all the marvelously recondite arguments have been adduced by the new pessimists of the social sciences, one may still suspect that their ideological convictions control their "scientific" judgments. The possibilities in political things are not as narrow as one's interests, fecklessness, and moral preconceptions may make one believe.

Moreover, if for any reason a person does come to believe that it is impossible to achieve even a partial democracy of participation, then that belief will diminish the likelihood that participatory institutions will in fact take root and grow. The Madisonian makes his wish father to his belief; and his beliefs partly create the sociological facts he conveniently predicts when he applies his "Iron Laws."

But the Rousseauan has an even more crushing response. There is really no need to speculate about these matters. For while skeptics speculate, the possibility of a democracy of participation is being proved by those who believe it to be possible and are acting on that belief. In the urban ghettoes of Chicago, Cleveland, and Newark, in the rural ghettoes of Alabama and Mississippi, young men and women with a vision are helping to forge new institutions undeterred by the theoretical cautions of their realistic elders. Moreover, the very pressure of need has generated "disorderly" surrogates for socially accepted forms of participation. Sit-ins, lie-ins, teach-ins, protests, civil disobedience, cooperatives, tent cities, freedom parties, petitions, legal action, poor people's corporations, community unions, mass rallies, wildcat strikes, and other social inventions are expressions of the need to participate more directly in the making of policies that vitally affect one's life. Nor has this proliferation of institutional devices for satisfying a felt need been fruitless. For the rhetoric of left-wing radicalism is being gradually reabsorbed into the rhetoric of American liberalism. Thus, with all its defects, the Poverty Program will have one achievement of historic significance to its credit. By administrative rule it requires that the poor, whom its programs are meant to benefit, shall have representation on the boards and committees that are authorized to administer those programs. Already liberals are beginning to think of other ways to apply this principle to the administration of public funds.

No doubt, this rule is honored in the breach. But the important thing is that for the first time in America's modern industrial era the right of participation in a form other than an occasional vote has become part of the rhetoric of public policy, and it initiates a new dialectic of disorder. Jeffersonian rhetoric may once again be heard in the conventional agencies of the land. Stodgy officials of planned parenthood associations, private welfare agencies, of legal aid societies, community action committees, educational associations, and of many other groups, private and public, have long and zealously guarded their prerogative to do good for others without being bothered by those lucky recipients of their largesse. Increasingly these officials are forced to respond in some way to the insistent pressure of those who insist on implementation of the policy decreeing participation by the poor. Debate and discussion, conflict and cooperation generate a new unfulfilled aspiration to participate—one that will not be satisfied by an occasional vote for members of a poverty program committee.

And in our colleges and universities, students no longer ask for the right to share in the vital decisions that shape their educational experience—they *demand* it. College administrations are beginning to respond to this demand. At

Berkeley and at the University of Michigan steps have been taken. At Tuskegee Institute, Booker T. Washington groans. The only brake on a more accelerated pace of change is that of the students' own fears and insecurities—in large part the product of the pseudo-realism with which their minds and spirits have been contaminated. But there is every prospect that at least the radicals among this generation of students will not be bought off. If they are, it will be primarily because the self-indulgence of their politics brings with it despair and capitulation to the forms of democratically irresponsible power they rightly loathe.

The Politics of Radical Pressure

The foregoing analysis points directly to a new politics of radical pressure that synthesizes in mutually reinforcing ways welfare politics, coalition politics, and participatory democracy—a politics of radical pressure which operates on the principle that when one of these three vital constituents of a total liberal strategy is formally absent or defective, everything, short of rebellion, required to provide informal substitutes for them ought to be done—but done *effectively*. Gunnar Myrdal has argued that the creation of participatory institutions lies beyond the welfare state.* He is wrong in supposing that the task of reconstructing social and political institutions should wait until the basic tasks of welfare politics have been completed, though he is right in thinking that the life of autonomous mind and spirit requires relief from the insistent pressures of abject biological and economic need. But morally and politically, the development of a more deliberative process of coalition politics, the growth of participatory institutions, and the completion of the welfare state are concomitant enterprises—none more important

* In *Beyond the Welfare State*, New Haven, Conn., Yale University Press, 1960.

from a theoretical point of view than any of the others, all three absolutely indispensable conditions of a good American society. (In concrete situations it is, of course, necessary to assign value-priorities. I have no illusion that acceptance of what has just been argued will result in invariable harmony when such assignments are made. My aim has been, rather, to counteract the tendency to focus so exclusively on one value that others are neglected.)

I say "a new politics of radical pressure." But this is misleading. What is really required is recognition of the processes that have proliferated and developed since Rosa Parks decided to keep her bus seat. This is the larger social meaning of the Negro revolution. What is also required is a more deliberate effort to use those processes more effectively in pursuit of radical aims. Sit-ins, freedom parties, teach-ins, and the like are surrogates for participation in the processes by which public policies are formed and from which those involved in these activities are normally excluded. (Often even from the pro forma exercise of the franchise, though this is admittedly in the process of rapid change.) My quarrel is certainly not with the existence or further exploitation of these social inventions. My quarrel is only with the supposition that they can be used effectively in any and all situations of legitimate social discontent. My quarrel is basically with pseudo-realists who eschew such tactics, and only secondarily with those who employ them self-indulgently. Whether tactics outside the frame of more conventional political processes should be adopted is not something that can be decided in general—on the basis of an incantation of ritualistic formulas like, "Protest, not establishment politics," or "Protest, not debate."

The strategic concept I am proposing is that of using any device, short of open rebellion or revolution, to bring pressure to bear in support of liberal aims.* But in any given

---

* Needless to say, I have the United States principally in mind in setting this restriction on strategic options.

situation the specific choice of tactics should be decided on the basis of that which effectively, and over time, tends to enable realization of the many values that a liberal seeks to foster. There is, from this point of view, simply no general case to be made for adherence to one preferred tactic or another. For there is no substitute for coldly reflective calculation based on knowledge of the concrete situation and comprehensive grasp of the entire range of liberal values we should seek to move toward.*

It is of central importance that every program advanced by radical liberals be so conceived that as many liberal values as possible are promoted; and, where they already exist, protected. Thus, for example, in advocating an extension of the War on Poverty, the liberal should demand not only that more of the poor be brought under the program, nor only that the poor be permitted representatives on local committees that administer the funds, but that the Poverty Program be used as an instrument for destroying those more conventional welfare programs that practice paternalism and breed servility; and that, wherever possible, it encourage a fuller participation by those the program is designed to benefit—not only in the administration of funds, but in the organization of the poor, in the development of leadership skills, and through giving top priority to experimental programs designed to foster fuller and freer community action.

Let us call the idea that has emerged from the preceding argument "the principle of the promotion of multiple liberal values." Given this principle, it becomes impossible to run, seriatim, through the list of evils requiring social remedy described earlier. Instead, the programs designed to remedy any should, within the limits of possibility, be designed to remedy all.

What shape might liberal programs take? This is not the

---

* Even given these ideal conditions there is a residual source of conflict that should not be overlooked. Two persons who have the same values may yet disagree about their relative importance.

place to apply the moral and strategic principles proposed in the foregoing to all of America's social problems. But in the last three chapters I apply these principles to the three problems that currently most agitate American liberals: Black Power, campus disorder, and Vietnam. It is these problems that make growing divisions within American liberalism most apparent.

6 AMERICAN
LIBERALISM
AND
BLACK
POWER

For about a decade American liberals and the more militant proponents of civil rights have enjoyed a kind of honeymoon. But emergence of the Black Power Movement has surfaced disagreements long latent within liberal groups—a fact not unfamiliar to black civil rights leaders.

Some of Black Power's liberal critics seem to lament little more than the slogan itself. More thoughtful commentators censure Black Power advocates for alleged abandonment of coalition politics. Still others view Black Power leaders as racist demagogues who aim mainly to foment violence and disorder. And underlying much of the hostility currently expressed by white liberals is a sense of virtue unrewarded— the feeling that they have given their all for civil rights only to be thrown on the scrap heap by posturing politicians.

Yet, when central tendencies of the Black Power Movement are viewed from the liberal perspective defined by what has gone before, it can be shown not just that those tendencies convey liberal themes but that their appearance is a triumph, not a failure, for American liberalism. For the advocates of Black Power have taken the rhetoric of liberalism more seriously than many liberals evidently intended it to be taken.

Theory and Strategy of Black Power

This can best be demonstrated by explaining the essential theoretical and strategic conceptions that underlie the Black Power Movement—not through interpretations provided by uncomprehending white newspapermen, but by attending to what principal defenders of Black Power say and do when they think and act reflectively.

We must first assess what the more conventional civil rights movement has achieved to date. Floyd McKissick, national director of CORE (the Congress of Racial Equality), has put it this way:

> The Civil Rights Movement . . . was concerned with the 10 per cent of the black people in this country and the Black Revolution [by which McKissick means the Black Power Movement] will be concerned with the 90 per cent who are not able to leave ghettoes for integrated neighborhoods because they are not mobile, for many reasons. They are trapped by society and downed [sic] for being trapped.*

It matters little whether McKissick is right in claiming that the civil rights movement was only concerned to aid a minority of Negroes. For it is certain that only a minority actually received significant aid during the last decade of effort. Even Bayard Rustin, one of the ablest critics of the

---

* "The Civil Rights Movement is Dead—Long Live the Black Revolution," unpublished manuscript.

Black Power Movement, admits as much and more. He writes:

> It may, in the light of the many juridical and legislative victories which have been achieved in the past few years, seem strange that despair should be so widespread among Negroes today. But anyone to whom it seems strange should reflect on the fact that despite these victories Negroes today are in worse economic shape, live in worse slums, and attend more highly segregated schools than in 1954.*

In other words, despite the Civil Rights Movement's many successes, considered in relation to the prodigious disabilities of most American Negroes, the surface has hardly been scratched. By and large it is those who live in the most segregated Negro communities whose lives have been touched least by the progress that has been made. These penned up multitudes can do little but huddle together in their ghettoes —the worst slums in affluent America. Whether they constitute 90, 80, or 70 per cent of all American Negroes is unimportant. The paramount fact is that this ghetto host does comprise an overwhelming majority. From their perspective the choice between more of the same and Black Power poses momentous issues about which men of equally good will may reasonably differ—or so I will argue.

To fully understand the political implications of the fact that so many have achieved the appearance, but not the reality, of meaningful human gains, consider the following question. What have more than three centuries of slavery, then serfdom, then existence in segregated communities dominated by White Power done to the typical ghetto-dweller? Before everything else it has caused what Stokely Carmichael describes as "psychological inequality." That is to say, too many of America's black citizens have been made to *be* inferior in wealth, status, and power, and hence to *feel* inferior

---

* " 'Black Power' and Coalition Politics," *Commentary*, September 1966, p. 37 (emphasis is Rustin's).

to their white masters. They have, accordingly, been made to feel dependent, to lack appropriate self-esteem and confidence in their ability to shape their lives according to their own deliberative choices. (Here I distinguish between pride —which such people have amply—and that adequate evaluation of one's self which is appropriate self-esteem.) In brief, though freed from slavery, they have not often enough been freed from slavishness.

The consequences of these conditions of the spirit are momentous. Feeling inferior, many have vented their inevitable rage on members of their own communities—the very people to whom they should be turning for consolation and for aid in their struggle. Jealousy and envy engulf some to such an extent that, rather than helping fellow black men to secure important public offices, they actually prefer continued domination by their white tormentors. They often deplore enhancement of status, power, or income that falls to a fellow black man. Conversely, those who do rise often guard their gains ruthlessly. Some even assume the white man's social role and manipulatively help to sustain an oppressive system by encouraging envy and jealousy. For this dominant whites reward them with effusive praise and modest emoluments.] Understandable fear also shapes such attitudes on the part of some Negroes. But it is difficult to distinguish such fear from envy, jealousy, or lust for high status. And there is this general truth with which to reckon. The pleasures of vain eminence require misery, and misery loves company—something that is true of all men, not just white men.*

And so life for most American Negroes moves in a circle that is literally vicious: odious conditions of existence produc-

---

* This situation occurs fairly commonly in the black belt of the South. Thus, not long ago, a well-qualified black candidate for sheriff in an Alabama county in which Negroes enjoyed an overwhelming majority was actually opposed in a primary by many leaders of the black community, though his defeat would have meant continuation in office of a segregationist appointed by then Governor George Wallace.

ing psychological inequality that in turn strengthens the very forces that oppress in the first place. The only way to make the flight from manliness even minimally tolerable is to practice deception—deception of the white man, but, above all, self-deception.

So it always is with human beings subject to tyrannical force they can do little about—as W. E. B. DuBois perceived, more than sixty years ago:

> Deception is the natural defence of the weak against the strong, and the South used it for many years against its conquerors; today it must be prepared to see its black proletariat turn that same two-edged weapon against itself. And how natural this is! . . . Political defence is becoming less and less available, and economic defence is still only partially effective. But there is a patent defence at hand—the defence of deception and flattery, of cajoling and lying. It is the same defence which peasants of the Middle Ages used and which left its stamp on their character for centuries. Today the young Negro of the South who would succeed cannot be frank and outspoken, honest and self-assertive, but rather he is daily tempted to be silent and wary, politic and sly; he must flatter and be pleasant, endure petty insults with a smile, shut his eyes to wrong; in too many cases he sees positive personal advantage in deception and lying. His real thoughts, his real aspirations, must be guarded in whispers; he must not criticize, he must not complain. Patience, humility, and adroitness must, in these growing black youth, replace impulse, manliness, and courage. With this sacrifice there is an economic opening, and perhaps peace and some prosperity. Without this there is riot, migration, or crime. Nor is this situation peculiar to the Southern United States, is it not rather the only method by which undeveloped races have gained the right to share modern culture? The price of culture is a Lie.*

What power and prophecy in this passage! But something has changed. Millions of American Negroes are no longer

* *The Souls of Black Folk,* from *Three Negro Classics,* New York, Avon Books, 1965, pp. 347-8.

willing to tolerate a life of deception and self-deception; of submission to White Power. In understanding how this change has come about we also begin to understand not only the principal triumph of the Civil Rights Movement and of that part of American liberalism that supported its achievements, but also the limitations on what conventional civil rights activity can, in the future, achieve.

For American Negroes are beginning to break out of the circle of viciousness. Suddenly many, not just the fortunate few, are prepared to undergo that psychological transformation without which equal citizenship in freedom is unattainable. And many who were among the first to enjoy the taste of freedom will not rest until all American Negroes are liberated. The rhetoric if not the reality of civil rights progress permeates the ghettoes of America. And, as always when there is a growing gap between expectations and the actual conditions of one's life, the dialectic of disorder begins to operate with relentless pressure to unsettle the lives of everyone: masters, slaves, and "innocent" bystanders alike. The result is a new leadership, prepared to exploit new possibilities. As Floyd McKissick has put it: "The process of freedom, itself, is a process of taking possession. It is also a process of learning. It is a process of growth, and the Civil Rights Movement gave birth to the leadership which is now able to take part in the black revolution."*

These developments are occurring not only in Black Power organizations. Within groups like the NAACP and the Southern Christian Leadership Council, the same pressures are being exerted from below; a new leadership is also emerging. All have begun to re-examine traditional assumptions of the Civil Rights Movement, the most important of which concern the desirability of racial integration and the politics of coalition.

Racial integration has been defended by the following

* "The Civil Rights Movement is Dead . . . ," *op. cit.*

arguments, among others. First, separation makes for in-equality; the "separate but equal" doctrine is a fraud. As Negroes are injured by segregation, they would surely be helped by integration. But second, segregation perpetuates racial prejudice among whites. Whites cannot become decent citizens until and unless they are forced to encounter their black countrymen in every sphere of social life. Both arguments are defective.

While integration may be a necessary condition of making better citizens of white men, it is far from sufficient or even particularly beneficial in many social circumstances. A wag once said that the surest way to destroy the stability of the international system would be to make sure that everyone really did understand one another. Similarly, in the short run, the forced integration of people whose general opportunities and prerogatives are very unequal is likely to confirm whites in their prejudice toward Negroes. It is improbable that whites, already predisposed to judge Negroes on the basis of criteria made for angels rather than men, are going to be particularly impressed by those who have suffered the consequences of three centuries of slavery and serfdom. For one thing, brutal oppression is not likely to develop charm, talent, or benevolence toward whites. For another, whites are not likely to appreciate the courage, sacrifice, and sustained effort required of Negroes who are willing to break the color barrier.

More important is the problem Stokely Carmichael articulated when he said, "In the past, white allies have furthered white supremacy without the whites involved realizing it—or wanting it."* As another SNCC leader, Charlie Cobb, once put it: "The one thing SNCC is fighting is white supremacy. We're fighting the paralysis that it has caused among blacks. We've got to get blacks to unlearn

* "What We Want," *The New York Review of Books*, September 22, 1966, p. 6.

that."* The Black Power leaders are chary of the subtle use made, even of programs like the War on Poverty, to perpetuate this psychological bondage. Their fear is legitimate; for whites, even the best intentioned of them, carry in their bones the cultural residue of more than three centuries of iniquitous exploitation of blacks. In many subtle ways whites express attitudes of superiority that are due partly to the fruits of greater opportunity, partly to the simple fact that social conditions have infected them with habits of command vis-à-vis Negroes. The morally regenerative impact of participation in the civil rights struggle can only begin to undermine such attitudes. If this is true even of those who harbor no ill will, what must be the case for those who do?

Couple these facts with others, already mentioned, about the feelings of inferiority, the lack both of self-esteem and of confidence in one's human powers, and we have the recipe for perpetual psychological bondage.

Think then what it means, for example, for a Negro youngster to be thrust forcibly into an integrated school environment. Floyd McKissick has put the point sharply. It is, he observes, a well-established fact that self-confidence rooted in control over one's destiny correlates very highly with educational achievement. Suppose now a Negro youngster suddenly finds himself in an educational community that does not want him, and is hostile to him when he arrives. What will happen to that child's "achievement motive"? It would not be surprising to discover, before very long, that he has become either a "dropout" or, because of "disciplinary" problems, a "pushout." "In fact," as McKissick points out, "total reliance on integration—which amounts to reliance on acceptance by the white man—is at direct odds with that sense

* In Andrew Kopkind, "The Future of 'Black Power,'" *The New Republic*, January 7, 1967.

of 'control over one's destiny' that . . . correlates so directly with achievement."*

This is not to argue that integration is never desirable. Quite the reverse—the virtues of integration have been amply described by those who believe in its power to transform men and institutions. What I have tried to do is detail one clear implication of the fact of psychological inequality on which the Black Power Movement bases so much of its analysis. That is, where such inequality exists, there is a presumption against integration's being meaningful or useful. The ingrained superiority feelings of whites encounter the equally ingrained inferiority feelings of Negroes. The result is additional despoilment of the human spirit. So, for the short run at least, integration is an underexamined, overrated goal of civil rights activity. Separatism may be a defensible tactic for the mass of American Negroes who will it so. At least, this is not a view that should be unthinkingly rejected by liberals—however committed they may be to integration as a long-term goal.

What of the long run? Here many proponents of Black Power part ways. There are many who suffer a kind of inverted racism; who are as unrelentingly antagonistic to the thought of integration with white men as many white men are to the thought of integration with black men. Yet in this, as in so much else in social affairs, human intentions are not ultimately the controlling factor in what actually comes about. For once the basic conditions of psychological inequality are removed, once the great mass of Negroes take charge of their own destinies, no doctrine of separatism will prevent the destruction of those institutional barriers that today separate American citizens. We have seen this happen on a limited scale. It must come one day for the entire nation. When we do eventually overcome, it will be in part because

* Letter to the editor, *The New Republic*, December 3, 1966, p. 35.

some have built integration's spiritual basis by mobilizing the ghettoes—even if their intention in so doing was racist.

This leads directly to my second point, about the politics of coalition. The leaders of the Black Power Movement argue that any political strategy yields too much if it sacrifices the prospect of dealing effectively with conditions in the ghettoes and rural black belt. In particular, unless the will to make ghetto communities self-determining is strengthened, there cannot be general passage from slavishness to self-esteem and confidence in one's own powers. For communal democracy, direct participation by and for black people, is the institutional key necessary to unlock energies essential to further civil rights progress. "The need for psychological equality," writes Stokely Carmichael, "is the reason why SNCC today believes that blacks must organize in the black community. Only black people can convey the revolutionary idea that black people are able to do things themselves."* And Floyd McKissick is even more explicit about the profoundly democratic significance of the notion that has given the new movement its name: "When we say 'Black Power,' we mean that black people must decide for themselves what they want and must plan and organize themselves to secure the necessary power to change their lives."†

But the redemptive work of democratic processes, an idea so central to the Rousseauan and Jeffersonian tradition described earlier, is not the only important consequence of communal self-determination. Theorists of the Black Power Movement see it also as the indispensable condition enabling America's black citizens to build their factional power so that it can be deployed more effectively than before within the Madisonian system of countervailing powers. In other words, it is necessary, or so it is argued, to forego some short-term benefits of coalition politics in order to build more

* "What We Want," *op. cit.*, p. 6.
† "The Civil Rights Movement is Dead . . . ," *op. cit.*, p. 10.

firmly the base of power without which significant gains cannot be made in the long run. And in so saying, the Black Power Movement's leadership is simply emulating what other ethnic groups have said and done—Irish, Italians, Jews, Poles, and indeed white Anglo-Saxons of the South. That is, the Movement draws a political implication from the facts of Negro powerlessness that Bayard Rustin described. Groups that lack power—political, social, and economic—are ultimately dependent on the power of others; hence, dependent on the politically problematic good will of others. We are seeing what happens to that good will when a society must choose between a war of pride and the well-being of its most deprived citizens. It chooses guns, slashes welfare, uses disproportionately large numbers of its poor to fight the war, and finds it politically inconvenient to do much to change this grossly inequitable distribution of the war's burdens. Thus, though the Black Power Movement inveighs against the rhetoric of coalition politics, the aim of participating more effectively within existing coalitions forms an important part of the rationale for Black Power.

Black Power and Human Rights

Self-esteem, confidence in one's own powers, democratic control of collective destinies—these are ideas basic to the liberal tradition. But, argues one sensitive and sympathetic commentator, Black Power marks a radical departure from the liberal tradition. For the older Civil Rights Movement pursued human values; the Black Power Movement pursues narrow group interests.* The point is misleading in two respects. The more conventional leadership tends to employ a rhetoric of universal values to pursue more effectively the narrower interests of Negroes as a group. The insurgent

* David Danzig, "In Defense of 'Black Power,' " Commentary, September 1966, pp. 44–45.

Black Power leadership tends to use the rhetoric of separatism in behalf of universal values. The underlying disagreement between the two is tactical and strategic, not primarily moral. Both contain admixtures of the universal and prudential. The more conventional leaders believe that their public pronouncements must be addressed primarily to potential white allies. The militants of CORE and SNCC believe that they must speak to the ghetto dwellers. I will return to this strategic conflict. At this point I want to drive home the claim that the Black Power Movement is partly, but importantly, motivated by a profoundly liberal and humane conception.

It is, after all, the Black Power Movement that has taken the most explicit and liberal stand on the Vietnam War—an issue that the more conventional leadership, with the important exceptions of such men as Martin Luther King and Bayard Rustin, shy from. The failure of other leaders to speak their mind is due primarily to their belief that public opposition to the war would adversely affect the interest of America's black men and women. Perhaps they are right; but it is the Black Power Movement's leadership that has been most vocal in condemning the war on grounds that it is immoral. That many white liberals seem to think that the older groups have a monopoly on morality, the newer ones being dominated by wicked self-interest, is primarily a reflection of their own class interests. In this, as in so much else, their political judgment is shaped by internal prejudices into whose hands their regard for higher values unwittingly plays.

In brief, underlying much that is said and done by members of the Black Power Movement is a passionate commitment to human rights; a fierce claim to be treated with respect; a desire to attain, in John Stuart Mill's words, "the dignity of thinking beings." These commitments are sometimes explicitly expressed by the Black Power Movement's leaders.

Malcolm X is one of the heroes of the movement. In his powerful autobiography, he describes his steady development from slavishness, to mimicry of white culture, to the strident racism of the Muslims, then, slowly and tortuously, to a standpoint most eloquently expressed in the following passage:

> Human rights! Respect as *human beings!* That's what America's black masses want. That's the true problem. The black masses want not to be shrunk from as though they were plague-ridden. They want not to be walled up in slums, in the ghettoes, like animals. They want to live in an open, free society where they can walk with their heads up, like men, and women!*

And Stokely Carmichael tells white men what the Black Power Movement intends to work for: "We are just going to work, in the way we see fit, and on goals we define, not for civil rights but for all our human rights."† The human impulse of these pronouncements was once agonizingly expressed to me by a Negro student up from the deep South. "Why," he asked, "are so many up here so phony? Why don't people let me be myself? And why don't they ignore my dialect and listen to me?" Why indeed!

These then are the mature statements made by "sectarians" of the Black Power Movement.

Yet it would be misleading to claim that the theorists of the Black Power Movement are simply good old American liberals. They are not. Nor should they be. For they are radicals. Their commitment to fundamental human rights is not satisfied by a parcel of laws that guarantees the form but not the substance of those rights. Rather they think that anyone who fails to do everything he can to implement rights violates them. From their point of view, the chief sin of American liberals lies not in what they do, but in what they do not do. It lies in the liberals' all too willing acquiescence

* *The Autobiography of Malcolm X,* New York, Grove Press, 1966, p. 272.
† "What We Want," *op. cit.,* p. 8.

to the institutional indifference that is the ultimate disorder in our blandly moral society. A revised structure of law and administrative procedure does little to create those human abilities, that will to do the moral thing, that fundamental reconstruction of our institutional order, without which the commitment to human rights is formal and self-deluding—a way of salving without saving one's immortal soul. In other words, the Black Power Movement's central criticism of American liberals is precisely the one being pressed in this book—that there is an enormous gap between the rhetoric and practice of most American liberals. And that gap is part of the trap, often unwittingly set, in which the typical ghetto-dweller finds himself.

Violence and Disorder

Liberal critics of the Black Power Movement deplore two of its supposed consequences. They claim, first, that the movement needlessly exacerbates the feelings of potential white allies; and second, that it irresponsibly promotes violence and disorder. The two complaints are not unrelated. For nothing so disquiets "potential allies" whose lives are relatively comfortable and secure than threatened social disruption. Are these criticisms of the Black Power Movement justified?

As for unjustifiable alienation of potential white allies, the issue turns in part on how much benefit flows from surfacing the enormous hostility and anger ghetto Negroes feel toward the white man. Malcom X's life provides an example of how the human spirit can work its way through such feelings if it is only given the opportunity. Martin Luther King, Jr., defended demonstrations in parts of Chicago where bigotry is most intense on the grounds that, in balance, it is a good thing to expose the hatred many whites feel for Negroes. What is true for these white men is true for black men. Those of America's black citizens who feel hatred for all white men will vent their feelings. That they do is not all bad. Until they do, meaningful racial reconciliation, meaningful integration of the races, cannot be achieved. The mere manifestation of fury is not itself to be condemned. Whites who permit understandable indignation at the black man's expressions of anger to cloud their political judgment are not, in any event, reliable allies in the struggle for civil rights. The real issue is *how* that fury is expressed. And this brings us to the problem of violence. For underlying most adverse white reaction to Black Power is the fear that its strident rhetoric, its impassioned advocacy of militant action, will release forces of disorder and destruction that every sensible person now knows lurk beneath surface "deference," "shiftlessness," and "laziness."

Moreover, it is the issue of the functions of violence that lies at the heart of the present division within the Civil Rights Movement. On the face of it, the question posed is whether it is permissible to carry weapons designed for self-defense in organized civil rights demonstrations. For no civil rights group denies the general right to self-defense, and no civil rights group advocates violence. But it is simply absurd to suppose that *this* is the issue that so strongly agitates activists within the Civil Rights Movement. Underlying this apparent conflict are deeper questions about the nature and functions of violence. And these more basic problems are so complex that reasonable men may disagree.

People committed to the civil rights cause lead an active fantasy life. They dream of violence—even the most moderate and responsible of them. A few years ago, shortly after the Selma demonstrations, I had a conversation with a Negro teacher who lives in one of Alabama's black belt communities. He told me that he believed it would be desirable for someone to assassinate a number of the more famous white bigots of the South. A SNCC worker who was present countered with the comment that vengeful acts would only invite retaliation against Negroes least able to defend themselves! A year later, when disorder came to his town, the teacher was among the most vigorous critics of those members of SNCC who, as he viewed it, were inciting to riot. Yet riot is a lesser offense, both morally and legally, than murder, and less likely to invite retaliation.

Not only that, but this same man energetically used the facts of disorder and threatened violence to help force concessions from a reluctant city council. The point is this. "Moderate" civil rights leaders who deplore violence understand well the political uses to which disorder, real or threatened, can be put. They know well that violence and disorder are bred by conditions of servitude. They implicitly acknowledge what their fantasy life suggests: that violence and disorder may, in some circumstances of American domestic politics, be a lesser evil. They also sense the relevance of what Frantz Fanon had to say about the problems faced by natives caught in an entrenched colonial system: "At the level of individuals, violence is a cleansing force. It frees the native from his inferiority complex and from his despair and inaction; it makes him fearless and restores self-respect."*

The basic disagreement between moderates and Black Power advocates is not primarily about the functions of violence and disorder, nor about the uses that ought to be made of social turbulence when it occurs. Rather they disagree primarily about the official posture the Civil Rights Movement ought to adopt toward violence and disorder. They also disagree about the working relationship that ought to exist between those likely to engage in violent outbursts and organized segments of the Civil Rights Movement. In this it is not at all clear that the men of "moderation" act responsibly. For by dissociating themselves from the ghetto forces that primarily threaten social convulsion they may do more to promote it than the men who relate to those forces in a positive way.

* *The Wretched of the Earth*, New York, Evergreen Press, 1966, p. 73.

Much violence and disorder is implicit in many demands for "moderation and responsibility." In many circumstances, and with the best will in the world, men who plead for moderation and responsibility become the mouthpieces of social forces that desire stability and order above all else— and who are even willing to pay a small price to secure social peace if doing so averts having to rely on the organized violence of the state. When those who threaten disorder heed restraining pleas, and gain nothing for their compliance, they feel betrayed. It does not really matter whether they are betrayed. It is simply a fact that the people for whom men of moderation and responsibility become mouthpieces seldom have any intention of conceding more than marginal reforms—a fire hydrant or two, a playground, a modest Headstart program. Hence, the angry ones, now feeling not only aggrieved but also double-crossed, are that much riper for violence. Nor is this all. The reality of marginal success actually whets one's appetite for cataclysmic action. What is achieved is not enough to reduce significantly the level of frustration and danger; yet it is enough to encourage the conviction that only by such tactics can substantial concessions be won.

From the point of view of those who are determined to protect unequal prerogatives and privileges, the alternative to minor concessions is repression. But given the circumstances that presently exist in the United States, this offers no alternative at all. Once the power of the rhetoric of aspiration has been released, and barring totally *unrestrained* use of repressive power, the day of judgment can only be postponed. That postponement will just increase the cost to everyone when that day finally comes. Better then *to be* responsible even if this requires that one no longer *seem* responsible to those who are invincibly "moderate."

White, "moderate" Americans must be made to understand that the degree of self-restraint they demand of black oppressed Americans is superhuman. That the latter sometimes fail to be superhuman is not surprising. Those who now claim that the movement goes too fast—is too energetic, too militant—were only yesterday complaining that Negroes are shiftless and lazy. When Stepin Fetchit suddenly begins to speak and act with violent energy in defense of his rights, white moderates begin to long for the days when Fetchit shuffled about, slowly doing the bidding of his white masters, drawling "I's a-comin'."

Who then is more responsible: those who try to relate to the real forces of the ghetto, who try to provide moral alternatives to violence and disorder, or those who stand aloof, using the fact of social instability to advance their political aims? Consider Stokely Carmichael who, in a speech he delivered in Detroit, said, "If you think I'm bad, you should hear the sixteen-year-olds in Chicago. The other day one called me a 'Tom.'" Is Carmichael more or less responsible than the moderate newspaper publisher who called him a "mad dog"* for trying to channel ghetto fury in ways that hold some promise of averting the worst kinds of violence? Is another SNCC leader who told me he wanted to spend his "time and energy in Negro communities building power, motion, and self-identity" more or less responsible?

And who is more responsible: those who ignite the tinder box that has been made of the ghettoes, or those who, through endless acts of neglect, have made those ghettoes the tinder boxes they have become? Negligence is, after all, something for which men can be held responsible. Moral responsibility is primarily a function of whether you know what you are doing, and whether you have the power to bring about decent conditions—notions that lie at the very heart of liberal respect for the conditions of a deliberatively shaped life.

* John Knight, the *Detroit Free Press*, editorial on September 11, 1966. Knight claimed that the information that justified his judgment was transmitted to him by Ralph McGill, publisher of the *Atlanta Constitution*. McGill, in turn, referred to the Atlanta disorders that occurred in October 1966. For a different view, see Paul Good's "A Tale of Two Cities," *The Nation*, November 21, 1966.

Where is one to draw the line between manly prudence and groveling deference to White Power? Only a morally arrogant man can presume to have an easy and conclusive answer to this ultimate and agonizing question.

A Strategic Choice

For a genuine liberal, what is at issue in the controversy about Black Power is a momentous strategic option. On the one hand, the Black Power Movement claims that the indispensable condition of eventually achieving the legitimate goals of the Civil Rights Movement is mobilization of the ghettoes. This is necessary, first, because it accomplishes a redemptive work required to remedy the terrible impact on the human spirit of three centuries of bondage; and second, to organize the base of power without which America's black citizens cannot function as effectively as possible within the conventional democratic structures. The advocates of coalition politics, on the other hand, reply that alignment with potential white allies is required now. For it is now possible to work effectively toward many, albeit limited, policy goals— better housing, more employment, improved educational opportunities, better poverty programs, and so on. They add that militant rhetoric and action which needlessly generate white hostility diminish black power to achieve desirable short-range goals—and Negro poor, like other human beings, do after all live in the present.

Confronted by this strategic option, what is the Civil Rights Movement to do? The obvious answer is, "Both!" Let there be a division of labor. Let some work to organize the ghettoes, with the sympathy and support of those who do not choose to do so. Let others work to exploit the presently feeble instruments of coalition politics. And let white liberals fit into this complex strategy in ways that promote maximum benefit, minimum harm. Just what concrete implications follow for the development of a politics of radical liberal pressure will be discussed. Here it is enough to emphasize that it is simply fantastic to suppose that, given the enormous disabilities of American Negroes, there is not enough for everyone to do. It is equally obvious that not anyone is well qualified to do everything. While this may mean that some of what Peter is doing will be undercut by Paul's activities, what Peter or Paul can do alone cannot equal what they can do together—separately perhaps.

Some Criticisms of the Black Power Movement

Does it follow that liberals are never entitled to criticize what is said and done in the name of Black Power? Of course not. It is not legitimate criticism that is at issue, but the barbs aimed from behind walls, thick and high, that shield white critics from full awareness of intolerable realities; that enable them to transmute concrete human indignity and human suffering into a "social problem" that requires a bit of "social action." The important thing is not to stir guilt, but to sharpen one's intellectual grasp of the immensely powerful institutional conditions that reinforce prejudice by promoting indifference. It is one thing to read a vague description of the ritual emasculation of an Australian aborigine; it is quite another thing to see the knife fall, the blood flow, and to feel what one would feel if he were present.

Young civil rights militants have a justifiable repugnance of moral rhetoric that has the effect of entrapping Negroes more completely than before. They even have an expression for the phenomenon; they call it "the trick bag." I hope and think the following criticisms avoid manufacturing yet another trick bag. For certain criticisms of the Black Power Movement are justified. And whether sound or not, they deserve to be answered with argument, not invective.

The claim that the Movement's leaders are often demagogic is one such. I once heard a leader of SNCC tell some poor ignorant rural Negroes that the murder of a young SNCC worker had been plotted by their city councilmen. He may have been speaking metaphysically. But the subtlety was lost on people who had been given no reason to believe that he meant what he said in anything but its literal sense.*

This sort of demagoguery does two terrible things. It exhibits precisely the same lack of respect for Negroes made vulnerable by tyranny that typifies their treatment by whites who never hesitate to use the "big lie" to maintain oppression. And it needlessly antagonizes allies, potential and actual, black and white, who respect the truth and think that it is part of their business as civil rights militants to serve it. Although there is no reason to suppose that black leaders will be more immune from the temptation to practice demagoguery than white adversaries like Wallace of Alabama or Perez of Louisiana, there is no justification for exempting black leaders when they too yield to the temptation.

But underlying demagoguery is often reverse racism. That it flows from weakness and legitimate indignation is not to excuse it. In this connection, what needs to be stressed is a point that Stokely Carmichael has repeatedly made—the difference between condemning institutions and condemning men. This distinction is not, however, always so nicely maintained during the hurly-burly of civil rights activity. That all American whites are implicated in institutional practices that maintain racial oppression is a fact. But it is an institutional fact that may legitimately be cried from the housetops without impugning the personal motives of any particular white man, many of whom do have good will, however difficult it may be for them to translate good intentions into politically meaningful consequences. Black racism does decrease the likelihood that white men will express their moral concern as political support. This argument may seem to conflict with

* See my article, "Murder in Tuskegee: Day of Wrath in the Model Town," *The Nation*, January 31, 1966, p. 124.

what I said previously about the importance of venting feeling and mobilizing the ghetto. But leadership does have special responsibilities, and it is important at least to try to strike the balance between the need to cry out against tormentors and the need to build strength that effectively serves the legitimate interests of those who mainly suffer the consequences of oppression. The point is, the Black Power Movement's leaders often display more self-indulgence than tactical shrewdness in their expressions of social hostility.

The question of the white man's motives is relevant to the problem of integration. I defended the validity of the Black Power Movement's claim that integration has been a much overrated strategic aim of civil rights activity. Yet many people, white and black, have a deep and healthy commitment to integration as a personal matter. And not just for the social good it may do. The idea that human relationships should ultimately be controlled by a biological accident as trivial as skin pigmentation strikes them as insanely inhuman. The idea that any black who favors integration does so out of the base desire to curry favor with "superior" whites; that any white who does so expiates guilt; these are stereotypic beliefs that have as much and as little of truth in them as the idea that all Negroes love rhythm, all Jews love money, all Irish love political power, and all French love love.

Further, the view that, for example, integrated education must harm the Negro child if the teacher is white; that it does not matter how incompetent and paternalistic the Negro teacher is, nor how competent and sensitive the white teacher is; that nothing matters but color and the "identity problem"; this is simply self-defeating nonsense. The *institutional* point about the harmful effects of much integration must be made. It is well made by theorists of the Black Power Movement. But to suppose that the general thesis holds for every particular set of circumstances is to permit intelligence to be engulfed by racial feeling. And who suffers the consequences when error is made? The youngster who is made a pawn in the outside struggle for civil rights, the inside struggle for personal integrity.

Indeed, in this matter, the Black Power leaders play into the hands of the meanest, most entrenched interests within Negro communities. For basic suppositions of the Black Power analysis are that centuries of racial despotism have left the Negro community depleted in technical and spiritual respects essential to human growth; and that many black men take advantage of the situation to feather their own nest, feed their own lust for power. These are malignant, brutal facts—but they are facts. For the leaders to ignore them may compound the initial evil in ways that hurt others more than themselves. Whites are not the only ones who are capable of serving personal needs by toying with the destinies of others.

I have also, on occasion, encountered a tendency on the part of leaders of the Black Power Movement to convert valid psychological insights into absurdly rigid metaphysical opinions. For example, one SNCC leader once seriously argued that the difference between the Black Mind and the White Mind is so fixed and unalterable that there is a Black Logic and a White Logic. Such a claim is painfully reminiscent of the nonsense Friedrich Engels and other Marxists spouted about dialectical logic. Well, the computer industries of Russia are based on the principles of good old Aristotelian logic. And the resources of the Negro community will, in the end, be most effectively developed on the basis of the same principles of *human* reason. To suppose otherwise is to throw baby out with bath water; to repudiate the hard-won achievements of human intelligence in a fit of self-indulgent pique. Whatever advantage for the ego of the group may flow from such metaphysical excess is more than counterbalanced by the extent to which it impedes the very effort to acquire the intellectual instruments that make group progress possible.

Finally, it does little good and much harm to exaggerate the differences between the Black Power Movement and those who defend the more conventional politics of coalition. To portray men like Bayard Rustin, A. Philip Randolph, and Martin Luther King, Jr., as sell-outs is to display an arrogance of powerlessness. Not only does it defeat the very aims the Black Power Movement purports to serve by supposing that there is only one true way, but it is intellectually incoherent as well. For in one sentence coalition politics is attacked, in the next Black Power is justified on the grounds that it helps build the power of Negroes to function effectively in American politics. If coalitions are eventually necessary to secure all the rights to which America's black men are entitled, why not a little freedom now?

The inconsistency is made plain by the fact that every major leader of the Black Power Movement endorsed the A. Philip Randolph Institute's *Freedom Budget.** This makes it clear enough that they endorse in practice what they deny in rhetoric—that coalition politics is one instrument of civil rights activity right now. Nor should they deplore the modest success Martin Luther King's organization has had in devising new instruments for mobilizing the ghetto of Chicago— for example, the tenants' unions that promise some help for Negro slums.

Having made these criticisms, it is necessary to repeat a point implicit in what has gone before. The sins of the Black Power Movement are mere peccadillos compared to the sins of omission of many "moderate" and "responsible" liberals, who think that because they do not deliberately corrupt they do not abet corruption. The difference between private virtue that is corrupt and corruption that knows itself is self-deception.

* A "*Freedom Budget*" for *All Americans*, A. Philip Randolph Institute, October 1966.

The Politics of Radical Pressure and Civil Rights

Given the analysis developed up to this point, what *liberal* theory of correct civil rights strategy emerges?

It is important to focus firmly on the two main aims of any liberal policy—*self-government* consistent with *protection of basic rights.*

The strategic points to be stressed are these:

1. Given situations in which Negroes are forced to choose between disorder and passive acceptance of their condition, disorder may be justified.

2. The aim should be to broaden the options—to provide alternatives and more constructive channels for destructive energies. This the Black Power Movement as well as other civil rights organizations are trying to do. The *Freedom Budget,* a 180 billion dollar program for eliminating poverty, is one step in a historic effort to get America to meet its obligations; to cope with the conditions that breed violence without resorting to repression. In addition to programs that are expensive—employment, recreation, education, and the like—there are less costly institutional changes designed to develop the priceless virtues of a self-governing people. It is these the Black Power Movement is primarily concerned to develop. All these programs, including those advocated by Black Power organizations, deserve the active support of liberals. Instead indignant white liberals have tended to withdraw support—financial, political, and moral—in a seemingly high-minded, but actually self-serving attempt to counter legitimately rebellious tendencies by doing the miserly thing.

3. Compensatory programs—especially in education, housing, and employment—provide white liberals with their greatest opportunities for creative civil rights action. But good intentions are too often paralyzed by a moral uneasiness

about the justice of reparations; an uneasiness that has the same roots as much ambivalence about Black Power. On the one hand, liberals feel the urgency of compensating black American victims of a system that has materially benefited most American white men. On the other, they feel the force of the formalism, "Treat everyone equally, and without regard to race." And, as so often happens, their moral ambiguity results in stunted effort, the achievement of tokens. But the liberal case for generous reparation for Negroes is overwhelming.

Millions of America's black citizens are *technically underprivileged.* Conditions of early development have deprived them of skills without which a good life in this society is impossible. It is not just that these skills are a key to material success; they also open the door to developing human powers without which life shrivels. Money is time and energy for love, thought, art, and play. The theory of this society is that, except for those who exit from the womb carrying inherited gold, access to wealth is primarily a function of the abilities required for success in competition. There is some truth in the theory.

In the United States, therefore, the ideal of equal opportunity requires the right to compete freely for available resources. And this right of free competition can be denied not only by obstacles that prevent us from doing what we otherwise have the skill to do, but also by alterable conditions that prevent us from acquiring necessary talents. Those deprived of competitive freedom because they have been denied opportunity to develop skills are entitled to compensatory social action.

This right of restitution may justify land redistribution, income maintenance programs, reverse discrimination in employment, housing quotas, and so on. Above all, society has an absolute obligation to insure that a father's disabilities are not transmitted to his son. Toward this end nothing is more important than educational programs designed to remedy the harm already done; and, when impossible, to bar compounding the damage. Top to bottom reconstruction of even our most prestigious educational institutions may be required.* To deal adequately with the educational problems of the technically underprivileged would be very expensive. But a nation that has commodities coming out of its ears can afford whatever is necessary to build people's minds and spirits. Beyond educational reform, agencies such as police review boards, created to protect Negroes from whites whose very habits of thought and feeling have unwittingly been shaped by the centuries-old institutions of racism, may be justified.

Even those who grant the general case for compensatory programs often object that, in designing them, there is no reason why Negroes should receive special consideration. They properly insist that many others have been similarly maltreated. It is true that, all other things being equal, Negroes ought not to be compensated in ways that disadvantage others who have legitimate claims—all technically underprivileged, regardless of race. Nevertheless, in the case of American Negroes all other things are rarely equal.

First, if Negroes, socially the lowest stratum in this society, receive reparation, the pressure to complete the process will be well-nigh irresistible. All the disadvantaged will eventually be helped. Indeed, one of the great ironies of the 1960s is that poor and working class whites—generally the most open in their actions and expressions of anti-Negro sentiment— are already profiting substantially from successful civil rights efforts.

Second, though Negroes constitute only about 10 per cent of the total population, they comprise approximately half the poor of this society.

Third, Negroes are the most glaring and easily identifiable victims of the processes that make for technical underprivilege. Not only has their victimization been far greater in

---

* The problems of higher education for the technically underprivileged will be discussed more fully in the next chapter.

proportion to any other segment of the population (with the exception of American Indians), but three centuries of American slavery have made their afflictions special. To postpone compensation designed to eliminate the black man's technical underprivilege until solutions are achieved for the complicated administrative and political problems involved in making such programs available to all who deserve them compounds present injustice in two ways. Rights already infringed are violated again because others also have claims. Where is the justice in that? Also, as the operative cause of racial injustice is racial prejudice, almost all whites have actually benefited from oppression of Negroes. This is true even of those who have been themselves badly treated. Thus, for example, poor Southern whites who have been victims of economic injustice have nevertheless used their power over Negroes to mitigate their misery in various ways—not the least being the pursuit of the pleasures of daily mastery.

For the reasons given, a program of restitution for America's black citizens is stronger and more compelling than it is for any other group save one. Nor should whites who try to meet their obligation expect gratitude for their pains.

As Frantz Fanon put it when writing about similar claims made by colonials against their former masters: ". . . when we hear the head of a European state declare with his hand on his heart that he must come to the help of the poor underdeveloped peoples, we do not tremble with gratitude. We say to ourselves: 'It's a just reparation which will be paid to us.' "* Few deny the German nation's strong obligation to compensate Jews who had somehow escaped Nazi genocide. Though the American nation's obligation to compensate American Negroes may seem less dramatic to many, it is every bit as compelling. For the difference between a German Final Solution that resulted in the extermination of millions over a brief period, and an indigenous American colonial sys-

* *The Wretched of the Earth, op. cit.,* p. 81.

tem that has brutalized millions over a long period, lacks moral significance. Both are heinous.

I have argued that the central tendencies of the Black Power Movement are liberal, and that the movement deserves liberal support. At the same time, the politics of radical pressure is best satisfied by recognizing the momentous strategic options facing the civil rights movement, and by avoiding "either-or's." Conventional civil rights activity has accomplished much; it has much yet to accomplish. There is plenty of room for people who, by temperament or aptitude, can do their best work in the new or the old. The important thing is that, in the midst of controversy, we do not forget that those who suffer needless internecine conflict are those who have taken the brunt of three oppressive centuries, and who continue to be oppressed.

7 AMERICAN LIBERALISM AND HIGHER EDUCATION

Today the big business of higher education is also big politics. California's Ronald Reagan made disorder on the state's campuses a major issue in his campaign for governor. At his inaugural his hint that established values were being subverted on those campuses produced the loudest ovation.

Like ghetto-rioting, campus disorder has deepened splits within the liberal community. For liberals are unsure whether these disruptions are tolerable, partly because they are not clear about the aims of higher education in the modern world.

Snobbery and Technology

Half a century ago things were easier for liberals. The basic clash over higher education was between snobbery and practicality. Some thought higher education was pointless unless it was useless; others that useless education was pointless. With lofty disdain Thorstein Veblen described the views of some who sought a classical education because of its "utility as evidence of wasted time and effort and hence of . . . pecuniary strength."* On the other hand, practical men viewed such "waste" as sinful failure to employ existing wealth to acquire more.

In Veblen's time, education for dilettantes had much the better of things. Institutions of higher learning managed to achieve the worst of two possible worlds. For people increasingly dedicated to the forging of a money culture, they produced the refinements of snobbery. And, to add emptiness to hauteur, American snobs mainly lacked the intellectual distinction and civility of typical English counterparts.

But technology's movement proved irresistible. It swept through and transformed American universities. After World War II American multiversities that had been in the making emerged as shopping centers for careerists. The prestige of classicists receded. Though higher education was still a commodity the possession of which was mostly restricted to those who could afford it, at least America's burgeoning industrial needs were largely served.

Conventional radicals too easily forget how dependent is the national society upon the university; dependent in ways that make possible their higher discontents. C. P. Snow, in his novel *The New Men*, describes a wartime incident, undoubtedly close to fact, that illustrates the point. Britain's new men were the atomic scientists who, during the early dark days of the war, labored to produce an atomic bomb. At one point they tried desperately to induce the government to permit assignment of thirty or forty more scientists to their project. Hard, drawn-out bargaining yielded authorization to add about half the number they sought. Shortly after this

* *The Theory of the Leisure Class*, New York, New American Library, 1953, pp. 255–256.

modest success, Pearl Harbor was bombed. "Then America came into the war," writes Snow, "and within a few weeks had assigned several thousand scientists to the job."*

Britain's present economic failures are in no small measure a function of reluctance to retool her educational machinery so that it could better serve her contemporary industrial needs. It comes as no surprise to men versed in the ways of industry that corporation executives trained for gentility, used to starting the working day at a decently advanced morning hour, lack the entrepreneurial skill to enable their country to keep pace with less class-ridden industrial societies.

I say all this to make it plain that though the criticisms of American higher education that follow are harsh, in making them I finger my ball-bearing rosary and count my technological blessings. Yet, in the shifting conflict between gentility and technology, the kind of higher education a liberal society requires, though celebrated in commencement rhetoric, has fared badly.

Liberal Education

What kind of education is that? Not surprisingly, a liberal education. For what is commonly called "liberal education" nourishes life freely and deliberatively shaped—the kind of life liberals cherish.

The enemy of such a life is unreflective belief and action; ignorance of what one is and how he has become that way. "Know thyself," the ancients urged. And their modern disciples echo their conviction. Examine the conventional wisdom; examine prevailing institutions; scrutinize whatever shapes life, no matter how sacrosanct it may be. Failing this you cannot know yourself. For before you examine that which has made you, you are largely the unreflective product of un-

* *The New Men*, New York, Charles Scribner's Sons, 1954, p. 46.

examined practices. To live freely and deliberatively one must take his life in his own hands. A liberal education helps the individual to do this by equipping him to examine his life and everything that molds it. It helps free the mind.

In so doing, liberal education threatens subversion of much that is conventionally revered—perhaps the state itself. But why not subversion that meets the test of reason, of reflective morality? Moreover, subversion threatened is not subversion practiced. "Criticism will arise," wrote Bertrand Russell, "only if the state is defended by obscurantism and appeals to irrational passion."* But if the institutions of the state, if other traditional practices and beliefs meet the test of sustained examination, then traditionalists who chance subversion will receive a priceless dividend. Whoever accepts a tradition after careful criticism will gain a more rooted, hence more meaningful and stable reverence of it. The idea that reverence requires mystery has always been a prejudice comforting to those who lack ultimate confidence in what they profess.

The liberally educated person is equipped to advance our critical understanding of things. Armed with "eternal truths" and truths more recent, invested with the disciplines of reason and with developed taste, he is capable of making some contribution to that cumulative product that consists of techniques, information, interpretations, artistic works, and theories that we may comprehensively label "human knowledge." Yet he understands the limits of disciplined inquiry in any sphere. He knows how even the most austere methodological convictions, the very ones that define what it is to be "rational," are influenced by interests, predispositions, modes of being that lie at the core of personality. The very notion men have of "reason" is affected by deep-seated needs and desires.

* "The Functions of a Teacher," reprinted in *Gentlemen, Scholars and Scoundrels,* H. Knowles, ed., New York, Harper & Row, 1959, p. 525.

A liberally educated individual also has an understanding of the limits of education—formal and informal. He knows that little can be taught, though much may be learned. He knows that such things as pleasures of sex, warmth of affection, and heartiness of appetite do not normally result from diligent scholarship or steady inquiry. Through education we can only diminish, never eliminate, the turn of the wheel or the turn of the screw as factors in shaping one's prospects for a satisfying life.

The screw's turn may, it is true, be abated by an education that fits one to fill, competently and responsibly, one of society's countless functional slots. And by making himself valuable to society, the slot-filler increases his "worth." Universities provide one with the means of attaining higher income and status.

Public Service, Pursuit of Knowledge, and Inverted Priorities

Unhappily, what passes for higher education in schools that devotedly impart technical skills has increasingly little to do with liberal education. The proliferation of special "professional" schools, the systematic impoverishment of the parts of the curriculum that serve liberal education in those schools, has accelerated the impoverishment of what is human in an education. The results are bad, not only for the individual, not only for the effort to fashion a liberal society, but also for the production of responsible and creative slot-fillers. For it is liberal education that is designed to enlarge the mind's range, free it of its tendency to move in conventional grooves, make it aware of and sensitive to the moral and aesthetic qualities of remote consequences; human traits upon which responsibility and creativity ultimately depend. Hence, liberal education is an *essential* component of the higher learning anyone gets—even engineers, army officers, and, heaven help the society in which this needs to be stressed, educators and social workers.

But the training of slot-fillers is not the university's only contribution to the public's welfare. Faculty members also serve as consultants to business, to government, to every group that seeks advice. On any given day, staff members of one of the great multiversities are likely to be spread around the globe, consulting. Or, less directly but no less importantly, they may be hard at work writing manuals intended to help those who fill society's functional slots to perform their tasks more efficiently and competently.

For these consulting activities, faculty members receive fees. It is never far from the minds of those who manage our universities that these sums help diminish the disparity between the base salaries academic personnel receive and the money they could earn in industry or government. Nor do administrators normally view as unwholesome the massive interpenetration of academic communities with business and political communities that results from consulting activities. Indeed, they are more likely to feel pride that public service is being provided than fear that the university's integrity is being compromised.

Besides liberal education and public service, universities have a third basic function—the pursuit of knowledge. I have already indicated that encouragement of the quest for knowledge, in an appropriately broadened sense of "knowledge," is a principal aim of liberal education. But, in modern institutions of higher learning, knowledge tends increasingly to be more narrowly construed, its pursuit more heavily institutionalized. The name given these narrower forms of inquiry is "research." Knowledge comes to be regarded as a commodity; the productive processes, an industry; and (it cannot be helped, the metaphor extends itself) the university in which these industrial processes are carried out, a knowledge-factory. There are basic industrial decisions to be made —which of the indefinitely large number of possible commodities to produce; what methods to use in producing them; how to market the products that come from the factory; and so on. Of course, all of these decisions are controlled by the aims of making a profit and building a career. Confronted by alternatives the decision-makers first ask: "Which alternative will help me to gain promotion, income, professional status, access to men of power and influence, social salience?" And second, "Which alternative will bring money, recognition, academic stars to the university?"

No doubt this description is caricature. The exceptions to it are many and important. The account does not begin to do justice to the scholar who loves truth and tries to penetrate mysteries because he wants to understand the nature of things. Nor have I described the other, more benign motives of those who "do research": genuine desire to serve others, theoretical commitment uncontaminated by careerism, effort to adhere to high standards of craftsmanship for its own sake. That is, the caricature portrays research as only a *job*. But for many it is a *vocation*. (The difference is this: the job holder works in order to acquire the means for living well; but for the man who has a vocation, his work is an integral part of the well-being he seeks.) For most, research is something of both. My purpose is not to impugn or neglect what is beneficial and noble in research, but to sketch institutional tendencies that increasingly prevail—and for the most part these are not good.

Some refuse to face the reality of these developments. Despite all evidence to the contrary, they blithely go along on the assumption that what is good for education is good for research, and vice versa; that existing evils are neither chronic nor irremediable.*

* See for example, *Education at Berkeley: Report of the Select Committee on Education* (more popularly called The Muscatine Report), University of California, March 1966, pp. 5–6. Also James A. Perkins, *The University in Transition*, Princeton, 1966. For an insightful critique of the latter, see Henry Aiken's "The American University: Part I," *New York Review of Books*, October 20, 1966, pp. 14–16.

Others face reality, but plead that sociological circumstances beyond anyone's control result in irresistible impulse. Rape is so clearly inevitable that it is impossible to resist the temptation to volunteer and enjoy it. Yet, there must be quiet moments when even these men acknowledge the extent to which they have violated intellectual ideals that do touch the lives of all scholars in some way and to some extent. Then, perhaps, one is filled with unaccountable remorse—like the woman in the well-known limerick, embellished to fit the case:

> There was a young lady from Kent
> Who said that she knew what it meant
>   When men took her to dine,
>   Gave her cocktails and wine;
> She knew what it meant—but she went.
>
> When asked why she lent herself so,
> She spoke, and her eyes lost joy's glow,
>   "My will merely bends
>   to pitiless trends,
> Though I seem to enjoy it, it's woe."

Perhaps despair is warranted. Some evils in life are tragic necessities. But then William James' wisdom returns to prick us. We wonder, are these things happening only because they are inevitable? Or are they happening in part *because* we *believe* them to be inevitable?

There is surely an entire structure of institutional rewards that promotes uncontrolled growth of unwholesome forms of research. If we assume these things are not inevitable, no magic wand of policy will wave them out of existence. There is no way to get at the evil except by dismantling, piece by piece, the institutional support given the existing inversion of morally appropriate priorities. And for one who can accept neither the optimistic view that research rarely interferes with decent education, nor the pessimistic view that it must inevitably interfere, there is the obligation to try to reverse what is happening.

A beginning can be made by emphasizing the centrality of the teaching function and of liberal education. For liberal education supports the proper aims of all forms of inquiry in three ways: by cultivating the disciplines of reason; by encouraging criticism of methodological fashions inimical to inquiry; by encouraging and supporting inventive minds.

The argument to this point supports this basic conclusion: *the quality of undergraduate education, and especially of liberal education, is the principal criterion by which the excellence of any college or university is to be judged.* Not only does the good life require this criterion, but its acceptance is also a most important condition of successful inquiry and of responsible and creative acquittal of duty by those who fill society's functional slots.

The other main functions of the university—public service and pursuit of knowledge—are less important than is a liberal education for undergraduates. But so far from this order of priorities actually holding in our universities, liberal education for undergraduates is typically the thing of least importance. That this is so is a principal cause of campus turbulence—a fact best appreciated in light of the somewhat conflicting claim that unrestricted growth of student enrollments is the principal devil in the piece.

Higher Education: Right or Privilege?

Worse, many critics of American higher education contend that the main reason for deteriorating educational standards is this rapid expansion. They accept an iron law of the debasement of quality through quantity; increasing numbers of students *must* result in worsening education for all. In their view all other causes of higher education's multiple disorders have little importance by comparison.

The tremendous growth of student population is due, according to the critics, primarily to the specious belief that all Americans have a *right* to higher education. Higher education, they insist, is not a right but a privilege which should be accorded only to qualified students. Already too many undeserving college and university students waste society's resources and bring countless evils to the processes of higher education. Unless the vicious trend is stemmed, today's still remediable educational calamities will become tomorrow's irreversible tragedy.

Not so, says John Gardner, Secretary of Health, Education, and Welfare in President Johnson's Cabinet. In an essay,* important because it is so representative of much current liberal thinking, he challenges important elements of the neo-aristocratic view just described. He flatly denies that mass education is necessarily bad education. America has the resources to maintain standards of excellence despite the present influx of students. It is her failure to employ these resources properly, a lack of the right kind of national will, that has produced whatever depreciation has occurred; not mass education. Moreover, Gardner contends, the country has an obligation to provide everyone with an opportunity to get the best education of which he is capable. Vastly more people are qualified than the nay-sayers would admit.

Yet Gardner agrees with the neo-aristocrats in one vital respect. He too denies that a right to higher education exists. Though he throws the net wider, he too insists that only qualified individuals should have the privilege of receiving one.

The existence of a universal right to higher education is denied by Gardner for essentially two reasons. First, many individuals are transparently unfit—the brain-damaged, the genetically incompetent, but especially the "slow learners."

* In *Excellence*, New York, Harper & Row, 1961, chapters VII–IX.

To "require" (this is Gardner's term) young people so afflicted to go to college would, however kind-heartedly, cause them more damage than their exclusion. Rejection for which plausible excuse can be conjectured is one thing. But to be tested and found wanting in a situation in which one has been stripped of saving explanation is needlessly destructive of self-esteem.

Gardner thinks that, on the whole, America is doing a tolerably good job of providing higher education to qualified persons. He admits that among the excluded "slow learners" are some who would not be so classified were it not for social and economic handicaps. But he quiets excessive concern by assuring us that for most of them, there is no convincing evidence that social handicaps are a major factor in their academic limitations.* Their disqualifying attributes are usually irremediable. Conversely, most qualified students are presumably getting a higher education.

Gardner also argues that the logic of the argument for the existence of a right to higher education would reduce the education given to its lowest common denominator—to the level of summer camp instruction. Note—Gardner does not argue that quantity as such would depreciate standards; only that efforts to educate the apparently ineducable would do so.

Summarizing his views, Gardner embraces a form of educational pluralism. "Properly understood," he holds, "the college or university is the instrument of one kind of further education of those whose capacities fit them for that kind of education.† For the unfit, other educational opportunities should be provided—vocational schooling, on-the-job training, and so on. Each of the different kinds of institutions thus devised can meet appropriate, but differing, standards of excellence. Only this pluralistic approach to educational opportunity can result in a proper valuing of human differences as well as similarities.

* *Ibid.*, p. 78.
† *Ibid.*, p. 80.

. Though Gardner's views are representative, they are in important respects defective. In probing the defects, the nerve of liberalism's family quarrel about the problems of higher education is exposed.

First, there is a simple, but important, logical confusion about rights in Gardner's argument. The fact that some people are properly denied the freedom to exercise a presumed right does not imply the right's nonexistence. The fact that someone may validly be prevented from freedom of political expression under an appropriately stringent "clear and present danger" doctrine does not destroy the right of freedom of speech. Nor does prohibition of ritual human sacrifice destroy the principle of freedom of religion. Human rights are always *presumptively* applicable to practical action. Exclusion of the brain-damaged from higher learning may be justified without denying that even they have a presumptive right to higher education. One may wonder what the functional point of upholding rights would be when exceptions of these sorts are allowable. The answer is that to maintain the right shifts the burden of proof to the person who denies that a given individual is entitled to higher education. And such shifts are often symptoms of revolutions in moral thought about social policy. We are, I believe, in the midst of such a revolution in American thought about higher education.*

A more basic objection to Gardner's views is that they suggest a defective conception of higher education. Liberal education is essential for the good life and, in general, liberal education requires higher education. That these things are

---

* A second flaw in the logic of Gardner's argument is the free and easy way in which he moves from acknowledgment of a *right* to alarms about *compulsion*. To claim that someone has a right to higher education in no way implies that there is justification to *require* that he exercise his right (*ibid.*, p. 78), or that he be "forced" to continue his education (*ibid.*, p. 80). For to have this right is to possess an opportunity which the individual may or may not exercise—as he decides. Indeed, to compel higher education would go some way to destroying its significance as a means of *liberating* people.

true is quite enough to establish a presumptive right to higher education. That higher education is increasingly also the means to higher status and income, and that those who manage our society are college and university graduates—both of which Gardner acknowledges—seems to clinch the case for the existence of this right. But Gardner does not think so. Nor does he have anything to say about the role of liberal education in higher education. That he denies the right and says little about liberal education suggests that he does not regard liberal education as an essential core of everything properly called "higher education." Gardner's radically pluralistic views about what kind of education people ought to receive deepens the suspicion.

In any event, it is not important whether my exegetical hunch is correct. For against the view Gardner explicitly takes I hold that, with a single class of exceptions, *every American is actually entitled to a higher education; because anyone is capable of being liberally educated.* The only exceptions justified are the irremediably brain-damaged. Given the present state of the evidence, and provided everyone gets adequate pre-college training, it cannot be convincingly argued that anyone else is incapable of benefiting from a higher education. The hypothesis is, in any event, one on which it is worth basing social policy for a century or two. Waste may result. But, to anticipate a point developed more fully later, it is far better to waste resources than lives.

The implications of this position are momentous. Acceptance would logically compel that the burgeoning system of post-secondary education—vocational schools, junior colleges, community colleges, whatever they may be—*ought to have the idea of a liberal education as the core of their program.* This by no means implies that different kinds of higher education should not be provided by different schools. For not every institution ought to do everything. But the different programs should build around a basic curriculum that has liberal education as its aim.

That anyone who is capable of benefiting from liberal education is entitled to a higher education points to another fundamental flaw in Gardner's position. It is simply not true that everyone who is able to benefit can, if he wants, secure a higher education. Millions suffer *remediable social disabilities* that bar them from our colleges and universities altogether. Millions of others either are not receiving an adequate education or are victimized by evaluative procedures that insure failure. Briefly, forms of discrimination inimical to the idea that everyone is to count for one, none for more than one, lace our educational system. The problem of racial segregation is but a small part of this larger problem of social segregation. A major cause of American society's failure to cope with what I have called the problem of technical underprivilege is prevailing social segregation.

Social handicaps suffered by the technically underprivileged are very great. Access to institutions of higher education, as well as access to the best of such institutions, is decided on the basis of evaluative instruments that are virtual instruments of class bias. Evidence mounts that criteria of admission and success within our colleges and universities are constructed, as if by design, to favor those who have already received the special advantages of affluence and a low-brow, middle-class family culture. It is as if the American nation is determined to maintain cultural mediocrity so that members of the middle class can preserve both high social status and the illusion of cultural excellence.

The discrimination built into present instruments for measuring aptitude and ability was impressed upon me when I taught in a small Negro college in the South. In a class of about fifty freshmen, one of my few Northern students—a young man from a middle-class family background who had received technically superior schooling—scored at or near the top of the class in all the conventional aptitude and achievement tests given. Yet he was my absolutely worst student when measured by all the criteria that really count—motivation, effort, ability to persist in that kind of sustained groping for understanding and intellectual independence that is central to higher education. Conversely, among those students who scored at or near the bottom of the class on conventional tests of aptitude and achievement were many who were very able—as capable of benefiting from higher education as any students I have ever had. Yet had these low-scorers tried, they would have been denied admission to schools much better equipped to serve their needs and desires than the one they were at; or had they been admitted, the probability of failure would have been high—so important are such technical factors as vocabulary, writing skills, general historical and cultural knowledge in securing the almighty grades required. Moreover, given the existing pattern of educational discrimination, it is undoubtedly the case that millions of such young people either fail to get into college or never try.

The evil results mainly from the fact that social resources for the type of pre-college education that might motivate and equip a youngster for college are allocated in ways that favor those who live in relatively affluent communities—suburbs rather than inner city, urban rather than rural areas, and, above all, any white ghetto over any Negro ghetto. The evidence is massive, compelling, frequently cited, and does not require repetition here.

Thus social segregation that already exists reinforces and consolidates itself in ways by which the lesser are made increasing to *feel* that they are less. I have already discussed this problem in connection with Black Power. But the same holds, I venture to say, for any group in relation to any other that enjoys higher social status—though surely not with the same raw severity and disastrous impact on mind and spirit that is true in the case of black ghetto-dwellers.

This initial pattern of segregation also tends to hold within our colleges and universities. For better faculty and greater resources, both public and private, tend to flow to the schools that are generally accorded higher status. Hence, the already disadvantaged go to inferior colleges and universities where they receive relatively poor higher education. This tends especially to be true for the processes of liberal education—the very aspect of higher education that should be of high quality for everyone, but especially for those damaged most by their early life experiences.

Low-prestige institutions of higher education, moreover, seem to be more paternal and arbitrary and to suffer more political interference than the high-prestige institutions. In other words, it is in higher education as it is in our social life generally: to him who has is given more, and the devil take the hindmost.

Beyond the vicious impact on the individual life chances of the technically underprivileged is the social harm done by social segregation. Although one cannot justify making each institution of higher learning a melting pot, there is every reason to create a socially integrated environment in which the true metal of each student can be discovered and refined. For it is only through constant exposure to others under conditions that show them at their best that the kind of mutual respect can be forged on which the strength and welfare of any social group ultimately rests.

I may seem here, by implication, to contradict what I said earlier about racial integration as an underexamined, overrated ideal. Let me make my meaning clear. I am allowing this exception to what I claimed previously. Negroes who are ready for higher education are, in general, more likely to possess resources of mind and spirit that enable them successfully to handle the inevitable tensions and social difficulties that efforts to forge meaningfully integrated communities require. Correspondingly, the probability is higher that white students and teachers will respond sensitively and constructively to problems that inevitably develop. They too will be afforded opportunities for growth. Higher education is, indeed, the main agency by which meaningful social integration can be achieved. In colleges and universities, more than anywhere else, the benefits of integration are likely to outweigh its costs.

It follows also that there is a strong case for compensatory programs in higher education. The historic injustices inflicted on the technically underprivileged suggest what the values of socially segregated education confirm—that institutions of higher education *should be redesigned so that conventional instruments of admission and evaluation do not reinforce class bias.*

Moreover, to do so may actually *improve* the quality of the liberal education received by even the most technically advantaged students. For by diminishing the extent to which reliance is placed on instruments that are educationally pernicious when used casually—"objective" tests, grading, and auxiliary paraphernalia—schools would be encouraged to attend more diligently to insuring that existing processes provide better education; on those conditions which, in Henry Aiken's words, "bring to the whole mind a fuller sense of its inventiveness, singularity, and freedom."* Viewed from this perspective, high educational standards depend on challenging students at the level of development they are at so that they can move to where they can be. Excellence is not primarily a matter of how successfully better-trained and better-motivated students are induced to take advantage of their educational opportunities; and it has nothing at all to do with requirements for admission. But these are admittedly large opinions about complex problems. I do not pretend that the arguments presented are decisive. My aim has been, rather, to suggest radical lines of educational experiment that are rarely considered, so pervasive is conservatism about these matters.

In the end, then, Gardner's views unwittingly exemplify the gap between liberal rhetoric and liberal policy that I am primarily concerned to expose. That those who attend insti-

* "The University II: What is a Liberal Education?" *New York Review of Books,* November 3, 1966, p. 23.

tutions of higher learning should have to suffer the anxiety generated by high standards is not in itself a bad thing provided that the tests are not unjustly weighted against them, and provided the basic tasks of creating qualitatively superior conditions of liberal education are performed. To worry that such experiences may adversely affect one's *amour-propre* is often rooted in paternalism or a desire to keep costs down and "undesirables" out.

It is, in any event, cruelly fraudulent to claim that high-quality vocational training, on or off the job, is morally equivalent to that kind of education without which a truly liberal society cannot be built.

But, just for purposes of argument, let us grant to skeptics that the experiments proposed will turn out badly. What will have been lost besides physical resources? Certainly the spirit of our people would not be damaged any more than it is by present arrangements. Given the actual conditions of uncertainty about how things might turn out, and viewing matters from the perspective of liberal *policy*, how much better it would be to waste national resources, even in a problematic effort to educate all our youngsters to the very limit of their ability for the kind of life liberals value, than to squander those resources in ways to which commodity-smothered Americans have become accustomed. For when every day is Christmas, the Christmas season loses all its meaning. From this point of view, the niggardly passion that starves education in order to maintain grossly inequitable standards of consumption is the original social sin that towers over all other iniquities inflicted by those who have too much power and affluence on those who have less of both than is their right. The time has come for affluent America to chance wasted resources, on however massive a scale, rather than chancing further waste of human lives.

Campus Disorder

The conception of higher education that has been advanced is one which has as its overarching goal a society in which every man is his own man. While society advances steadily toward a future in which everyone will have a place, colleges and universities are decreasingly able or willing, unable in many cases *because* unwilling, to provide conditions of adequate liberal education. This neglect is a main cause of campus disorder. For liberal education has never been a matter of such urgent practical concern to so many. Let me explain.

Despite a gloss of religious rhetoric, most Americans have been raised in the expectation that once America became the productive cornucopia it could be, each would achieve a secular salvation. But affluence has not proved redemptive. The resulting disillusion has been greatest among those who have always known a life of relatively great affluence—the present students, by and large, in our colleges and universities. (At the University of Michigan and the University of California at Berkeley the median family income of students is about $16,000 per year. And these are the two major *public* universities in the land.)

When the receipt of what passes for grace does not result in salvation, one begins to question the efficacy of grace—and to diagnose its failure. That is, social criticism and self-criticism become congenial to the very individuals who participate most fully in American wealth. It is wrong to suppose that they are motivated primarily by a burning desire to remedy injustice. Their concerns are at least as intensely personal and prudential.

Most of them come to the university expecting that there, at last, they will be initiated into the mysteries of rich and satisfying experience so bafflingly denied them in their prosperous family life. They find instead a community in which their expectations are not fulfilled. They find an agency in which research, public service, graduate education, and undergraduate education are valued in that order of declining priority; in which careerism is rampant; in which many of the most distinguished faculty members never teach undergraduates; in which conformist accommodation to power is rewarded, and authentic thought and action penalized; in which money talks—especially federal money; in which the gap between commencement rhetoric and educational practice is enormous; in which commitment to scholarship and research provides a rationale for political irresponsibility; in which, above all, basic decisions about educational processes and about the nonacademic lives of students are made by men who know little and care less about these things. Students study their university's master plan with dismay:

"So who needs nine-story classroom buildings, TV, and machines that will supposedly do the teaching," said the president of student government at the University of Buffalo. "There isn't a word in all this plan about us, here, now, and the needs and aspirations of students over the next few years."*

Under these conditions students who uncomplainingly knuckle under are sheep. They betray dispositions not fit for those supposed to be in training for freedom. Many students see the corruption of the university as merely symptomatic of the disorders of "the system," the hated "establishment." The university is simply its most visible, proximate part. So, frustrated by university life, they turn against it—and raise all kinds of hell. Campus disorder, more than any other factor, has caused faculty to pay attention to legitimate student gripes they typically ignored. The result has been new educational ferment; new willingness on the part of many at

* Ronald Gross and Judith Murphy, "New York's Late-Blooming University," *Harper's Magazine*, December 1966, p. 94.

least to think about ways of improving the quality of under-graduate education.

Though much of the "hell" students raise is directed against the university, and much is aimed at nothing very specific—panty-raids, LSD parties, orgies, and so on—students also raise much political hell. They use the campus as a base of operations for guerilla raids against a society they regard as mean and oppressive. And many of their complaints against the university have to do with the relationship between institutions of higher education and intimidating political forces in the larger society. Their political involvement is partly due to the fact that their personal distress and long exposure to the rhetoric of American idealism make it particularly easy to fire their moral imaginations. An intense repugnance is evoked by a society that seems increasingly bent on defeating human expectations here and abroad.

Their youth, moreover, permits them to see the reality of their lives and their society. Their need to protect bad investment of their energies by means of illusion is not as insistent as it is for someone who has spent the better part of his life in solid and respectable folly. Student perceptions are not yet so contaminated by the responsibilities of careerism. They realize that the celebrated wisdom that comes with age is more likely to make defeat tolerable than to make struggle for a human existence urgent.

Finally, today's students see more clearly than ever how the political myth of university neutrality is used to inhibit political activity harmful to the university's narrowest interests; to see more clearly the innumerable ways in which the university daily violates professed neutrality to gain educationally irrelevant advantages.

The Myth of the Neutral University

This last point is important because it raises the fundamental question of the university's political role. The issue sizzles on campuses across the land because of the special problem presently confronting university students—military draft during an expanding war. The draft poses a problem that puts students in an agonizing bind between self-interest and the sense of justice. Almost no one likes the idea of jeopardizing his life in a war that few strongly support. Most hate the idea. But all recognize that at present the burden of the fighting has fallen on those who have the least stake in its prosecution or successful completion. They fully understand that the civil war slogan, "The rich man's money against the poor man's blood," has its counterpart in the present conflict—"The rich man's education against the poor man's blood." Thus the same students who seek every legal way possible to avoid the draft bitterly protest the injustice of present selective service practices—injustice about which they feel all the more deeply because successful avoidance contributes to its growth. They are filled with a special kind of moral anguish and a correspondingly intense frustration and anger. They condemn a predicament they had no part in making.

They protest the draft. And they protest the university's compliant involvement in the operations of the selective service system. The university responds to their complaints by coolly proclaiming its political neutrality. Their school, the students are assured, is merely their agent in their efforts to avoid the draft. To the extent that this is true, it only intensifies the anguish. For students know that acquiescence, though serving their interests, also enables the university to avoid challenging the system that feeds it. They recognize that, functionally, the university disclaimer is partly fraudulent.

The students see that the pose of university neutrality in connection with the draft is but an instance of a more general tendency to employ the guise of political neutrality in order better to serve political masters. The university is, in all things, neutral; but in some things more neutral than in others. In nothing is it more neutral than when federal money is dangling. And federal bait is plentiful. Clark Kerr, deposed president of the University of California, points out that of the sums expended for university research in 1960, 75 per cent came from the federal government, 15 per cent of total university budgets.*

So universities have been neutral on the side of the CIA in some matters; neutral on the side of military training in others; again neutral on the side of the government's desire to exclude "subversives" from federal fellowships; neutral once more in performance of secret research for the Defense Department. The power that federal money vests in the university is but a fraction of the latter's growing power to affect people's lives. Under these circumstances it is inevitable that all interested parties will scramble for control of the growing concentration of university power; they will try to use the myth of university neutrality for their special purposes. Administrators are seldom more likely to be engaged in ideological talk than when they proclaim their university's political neutrality.

Given the existing fight for its power, it is nonsense to suppose that the university can remain politically neutral. No nation of democrats will permit it. Those within the university who think otherwise are like the government officials Thoreau once described as "standing so completely within the institution, [they] never distinctly and nakedly behold it."†

* *The Uses of the University* (Cambridge, Mass.: Harvard University Press, 1963), p. 53.
† *Civil Disobedience, in Thoreau: Walden and other Writings*, ed. Joseph Wood Krutch (New York, Bantam Books, 1965), p. 102.

The only question that is open is whether universities should brave the inevitable and at least strive to be neutral. Ideally, I think not. Universities should instead encourage skepticism of official action, promote social criticism and dissent, do whatever is consistent with the university's basic functions to reinforce committed, thoughtful, political action. In a phrase, make trouble for the complacent and the powerful if their complacency and power are undeserved.

The role is already implicit in the idea of liberal education with its stress on the importance of the examined life and the examined society. But there is an important, independent line of argument for a conception of the university as an agent of social criticism and, the inevitable consequence, social change.

John Stuart Mill once argued that every society should contain "some minds in which caution, and others in which boldness, predominates."* Both are needed so "that the tendencies of each may be tempered, insofar as they are excessive, by a due proportion of the other."† However, in any society the forces making for caution and conservatism are very powerful. In these groups power and motive coincide to inhibit radical thought and action. In the United States the creature needs of so many are actually satisfied that conservative humors fill every pore of the social organism. Yet, as Mill suggests, both social utility and social justice require encouragement of reflective but bold minds; of willingness to take the ax to the root if doing so can be justified.

Universities are particularly well-suited to help fulfill this need. Despite the criticisms made before—these are relative matters—proportionately more individuals devoted to the life of reason are to be found there than anywhere else in society. Those in university life who become thoughtfully radical are less subject to retaliation than almost anyone else in American society. In the past few years, for example, the Supreme

* *Representative Government*, the Library of Liberal Arts, p. 23.
† *Ibid.*, p. 23.

Court has seen fit to build protection of academic freedom into the nation's basic law—most notably in the decision that struck down the entire New York teacher "loyalty" program.*

Unless the university community itself acknowledges the social utility of politically bold minds, unless that acceptance is translated into institutional support, unless the arts of reasoned social criticism and the will to dissent are positively encouraged, the kind of political involvement described cannot flourish.

To claim that the university ought to encourage "the seeds of strange thought" is not to claim that it should serve any particular ideology. Socratic audacity is not an ideology. It is first, as Mill suggested, a temper of mind, a set of inclinations, a capacity for daring to question the conventionally inviolable. If this temper of mind is coupled with dissatisfaction about basic social arrangements, the result must be radical politics. So be it. For the idea that the university can encourage such a temper of mind, and yet should contain its political consequences for the sake of image and budget, is a fantasy that will appeal only to those who do not understand that thought and action must be a seamless web or creative thought about society must perish.

It is again worth emphasizing that radicalism is not entailed by the political role described. For established beliefs and institutions that run the gauntlet of sustained, reasoned scrutiny must acquire strength and resilience they can gain in no other way. And in a society which has few institutional flaws, general strengthening of conservatism would ironically result from a process designed to promote bold thought. In any event, conservatives who have a sporting instinct and the courage of their convictions ought to be willing to help construct a tough-minded testing process for their ideas.

Teachers have a special role to play in the processes which build thoughtful, meaningful political commitment. Univer-

* *Keyishian vs. the New York Board of Regents*, January 1967.

sity students are at the time of life when they actively seek
exemplars on which to model themselves. This is true of even
the most renegade student radical. Moreover, because a basic
aspect of the relationship between student and teacher is un-
avoidably one of power and authority (the teacher evaluates,
recommends, approves changes, counsels, has teaching assist-
ants, grants fellowships, gives the "answers"), the student
has a tendency to endow him with virtues larger than life—
infinite knowledge, *miraculous* eloquence, *absolute* integrity.
It is, after all, useful to suppose that those who have such
authority and power over one's life are perfect and incor-
ruptible. But let the teacher be thought to betray the
mind's-eye construction he has become by even a jot or a
tittle, and he lies in ruins, a shattered fink. That the fault
may lie mainly in the construction rather than the man is not
considered.

Hence, the hard truth is that, in the processes by which
universities promote boldness and commitment, the teacher
will have a specially heavy obligation to display, in his own
behavior, the ways in which intelligence and commitment
can be welded and translated into political action. He has,
somehow, to show that the life of reason need not be a life
of endless, impotent deliberation. He must understand that
omitted action *is* action; it too has consequences. He must
recognize that infinite tolerance of evil that only afflicts
others is the spiritual root of that impersonal, institutionalized
indifference that is the ultimate disorder in our morally
bucolic society.

At the same time, one must maintain perspective. I have
been discussing *one* function, not *the* function, of the
teacher. He is also public servant and investigator, and he
educates in other ways. From this point of view, the teacher's
political obligations are subordinate—but still important. The
strength of a teacher's obligations to play the kind of political
role specified is importantly related to his field of interest.
It is easy enough to appreciate why an ichthyologist might

think that his political obligations are unrelated to his main scholarly interests. It is impossible to appreciate why a political theorist should think so. And there is everything in between.

Teachers who try to meet the obligations described experience a special difficulty. Responsible action of any sort requires skills that are gained in detachment from the world of powers and commodities. Yet application of those skills to cases forces the teacher into that dirty, tumultuous world. The result is one of the tragic ironies of American education. Though incessantly urged to equip the young to make significant and responsible contributions as citizens, teachers who take their obligation seriously and try to fulfill it with integrity manage to generate massive institutional hostility and restraint. For those who suffer such consequences the experience is often devastating. Many teachers try, fail, and quietly subside; many more never make the initial effort. All comfort themselves with the thought that scholarship and pursuit of truth are nobler than social and political action—less distracting and painful besides. And there is much truth in their beliefs.

Thoreau also claimed that "a corporation of conscientious men is a corporation with a conscience."* The multiversity is living, sprawling proof that in this he was mistaken. There academic men of deepest conscience—men of private virtue—live and labor. They think, discuss, write, and give their last full measure for the committee of their choice. They are, in all things intimate, unfailingly conscientious and concerned. And yet, their very conscientiousness is used to rationalize abdication of social and political responsibility. "Private virtue; public vice," is the warning that should be inscribed on their office doors. Is it any wonder that when young men and women, searching for models, discover this reality, they are enraged and become ripe for participation in guerilla raids against forces within and outside the university that they

* Thoreau: *Walden and other Writings, op. cit.*, p. 86.

view as the embodiment of the established evil they find so revolting?

The alternative is this. Students and faculty should be given the widest possible latitude to act on the basis of thoughtful commitment. One practical implication is that use of the university's resources for political purposes is an appropriate part of its total program. Narrow notions of a special range of activities that are properly "educational" are illegitimately restrictive. In particular, the classroom is not the sole sacred theater of higher education; nor are a faculty member's classroom obligations to be equated with his teaching obligations.

The story is told of a dean at a midwestern university who had gained a considerable reputation for his skill in steering a turbulent campus through its first teach-in. An official of an Eastern university phoned to ask the dean whether he thought it proper to provide college facilities free of charge to students and faculty who were planning a teach-in on the Eastern campus. The dean suggested that unless his Eastern friend had lost his mind, he had better not be sticky about meeting the request. Did they want a riot? The dean's advice was good, but not the reason he gave. Use of college facilities for teach-ins and the like is justified, not primarily because that is the way to avoid trouble but because teach-ins are activities that can serve *legitimate university functions*.

In so arguing I am fully aware that to act on such a conception is politically perilous; and that, in any event, governance of the university is at least partly, but properly, the job of public representatives who do not usually find such a conception of the university's political role congenial. But I am sketching an idea at which it is proper to aim. To the extent that those who are charged with responsibility for governing the university feel justified in stopping short of the ideal for expediential reasons, let them do so. But at least let them understand that not everyone is in their position. To expect those not in command positions always to take the point of view of those who are, is to encourage role-playing* that does not serve the university well. For if everyone within the university community thinks and acts as if he had to deal with a legislative committee, where would the pressure for desirable change come from?

A Constitution for the University

Growth of university power has promoted campus disorder in still another way. Those affected by the use of that power seek to determine not only how it will be used, but who will possess it. It is not surprising that specific political controversy between students and administrators slides very quickly into protest about the right to participate in making university decisions. The focus of protest shifts from the specific grievances that precipitated action to demands for changes in university organization.

To see what role students can properly play in governing a university, it will help to describe in a sketchy way a constitution that might serve as a basis for rather fundamental reorganization of the university.† The suggestions are intended not to settle matters but mainly to provoke reconsideration of existing arrangements; as a first, very tentative, word, not the last word, about university organization.

The power center of university life is today clearly the administration. This is due in part to historic abdication of responsibility by both public and faculty. Ironically, both have scapegoated administrators in ways that have made it

---

* Cf. supra, pp. 30–32, for a discussion of role-playing.

† For simplification subsequent remarks are addressed only to the problems of organizing the larger, mainly public, universities. I am fully aware that the suggestions I make require modification before they can properly be applied to very different kinds of colleges and universities; though the difference between large public institutions and large private ones is fast diminishing. For both are "Federal Grant Universities," a phrase Clark Kerr employs in describing the institutions of "the multiversity," another of the expressions he coined.

easier for the latter to concentrate power in their hands. For the abuse that is heaped on administrators from all sides strengthens their conviction that they are doing something right; that they are the custodians of the idea of the university, when in fact they are protecting only their idea of the university. They like to think of themselves as benevolent mediators (Clark Kerr likens college presidents to clerks of meetings for Quakers*), even while they play a skillful game of balancing external publics off against internal university factions, the better to enhance growth of their own power and status. Thus administrators who should be mere *perfunctionaries*, as indeed they usually are in all but power, acquire a taste for their enhanced prerogatives. They resist, often manipulatively, threatened erosion of their control of university affairs—all in the spirit of benevolent concern for the welfare of the university's *basic community*; that is, students and faculty.

The starting point for any sensible discussion of university organization ought to be acknowledgment of the public's right to participate in the decision-making processes. Not only are general tax funds increasingly important sources of the money universities need, but, more important, the lives of all Americans are increasingly affected by what goes on in institutions of higher education. This last is enough to create a presumption in favor of participation by representatives of the public in the affairs of any university. This is so even if public participation threatens to retard advance toward the ideal of a university. The name of the democratic game is willingness to risk certain values for the sake of other more important ones.

The evils of public involvement have, however, been exaggerated. Much of the damage done by public members of

* *The Uses of the University, op. cit.,* pp. 39–40. John Weiss has provided a very perceptive alternative account of related matters in his article, "The University as Corporation," in *New University Thought,* Summer 1965, pp. 31–45.

the governing boards of universities is partly due to the fact that these boards are often not sufficiently representative; partly to the fact that the way they function facilitates artful manipulation by administrators. A political alliance between the basic university community and legitimately concerned publics based on common interests might go some way toward diminishing administrative mischief. Though this claim may seem wildly optimistic, there are supporting considerations.

For one thing, as more of America's young men and women pass through its universities, the potential for a politically significant demand for better education increases. The potential can, however, be realized only if members of the basic university community develop and more vigorously broadcast their ideas about better education. At present they do so only reluctantly, leaving the field largely to administrators.*

Members of the general public tend to be more ambivalent about the ideal of liberal education than is normally supposed. Even anti-intellectuals pay subtle tribute to the power of this ideal, for the hostile effusions of anti-intellectuals usually contain more than a little juice from the sour grape. And those who explicitly talk as if higher education is exclusively a means of securing more income, status, and power, do often resonate, however ambivalently, to its promise as a means of achieving richer human experience.

Finally, good education forces and the technically underprivileged, the very groups whose interests are least represented on the governing boards of universities, have a common cause. For, if my earlier argument is valid, the conditions of qualitatively superior higher education can be the conditions most likely to repair damage caused by defective primary and secondary education. The quality of a school is

---

* Witness the recent spate of books about the significance of higher education by university presidents. Besides the books by Clark Kerr and James Perkins (Cornell), there is Harlan Hatcher's (University of Michigan) *The Persistent Quest for Values: What Are We Seeking?* Columbia, Mo., University of Missouri Press, 1967.

determined by the excellence of its educational processes, not by its standards of admission. And there is no convincing evidence that excellence depends upon admissions standards.

Though the public has a right to participate, it does not have a right of exclusive formal control of universities. Yet governing boards are typically composed solely of members drawn from publics other than the basic university community. However, as faculty and students are the individuals most directly affected by decisions of university policy, they too have some participatory rights. Ideally, they are entitled to significant representation on their university's governing board. Presence of members of the basic community would help diminish danger inherent in participation by representatives of external publics. For joint membership on a university's governing board is a way of institutionalizing firm channels of communication that rarely exist. To the extent that this happens, the public would at least be better informed about the conditions of qualitatively superior higher education, the vacuum that permits administrators to harness power would be partially filled.

If governing boards are *working* bodies, if membership is not, as is so often the case, the prestigious perquisite of an individual who happens to have made his way in industry, the professions, politics, or High Society, the effect on the present status and power of university presidents would be decisive. A president would have to depend for his influence on the force of his personality, the quality of his arguments, the integrity of his commitment to a worthy ideal of higher education. Stripped of power and institutional status, good rather than predominantly ambitious men would be more likely to become university presidents than is true today.

University fiscal arrangements are also sorely in need of revision. At present operating funds must be secured annually from legislatures, other public agencies, or private foundations. The consequences are educationally pernicious. A university ought to be able to plan five or ten years ahead with reasonable assurance that its fiscal needs will be met. Yearly review and adjustment would not be precluded; but implementation of basic policies would no longer be dependent on the outcome of those deliberations. Thus, for example, the chaos that has resulted from the large-scale influx of university students everyone anticipated but no one adequately planned to receive was entirely avoidable. The population of our colleges and universities is expected to double in the next decade. Unless this growth is adequately financed, those who are disturbed by present disorder on our campuses will have to be carted to mental institutions in vans.

The controlling agencies of the university should have the basic say as to how the funds they receive are allocated. The system of grants for specific research projects, specific professorial chairs, or specific buildings ought to be held to barest minimum. The fact that the public is well and democratically represented on the governing board, together with the latent power to control that must always reside in the larger community, will assure that over time legitimate social needs will be met.

Freedom from constraining fiscal arrangements could be increased by establishing a system of counterpart federal and state appropriations. The federal government will, as it has and should, become an increasingly important source of funds. Through a system of matching grants to the university's general operating funds the threat of educationally pernicious intervention by state and federal governments can be mitigated.

If fiscal reforms along the lines described were combined with the organizational proposals made, the result would be to diminish further the strategic power of key administrators. For much of that power derives from their activities as fundraisers and guardians of the public's purse.

Student Power

We return, finally, to the problem that has contributed to much current campus discontent—the right of student participation in the decision-making processes of their universities. To understand why students should have a greater say in making university policy than they normally do is to bring into focus all the threads of the preceding discussion.

First, student participation is both an important part of a liberal education and excellent preparation for their assuming the roles of citizen, leader, and occupant of countless other functional slots. Individuals do not become responsible until they exercise responsibility. What better place to begin than in the university? Those who complain about student irresponsibility should not be permitted to have it both ways; to insist that students are not capable of acting responsibly, and yet to blame them when they do harmful things. The way one learns to be responsible is to possess decision-making power, to act, make mistakes, and suffer the consequences.

Second, students are an important source of information and opinion relevant to determination of the university's academic program. Few are in a better position to judge the quality of courses, the performance of teachers. Yet student expertise in this area is rarely sought; and when it is, it is secured in ways least likely to encourage responsible judgment. Consequently, despite a great deal of rhetoric about the importance of teaching, academic rewards are largely assigned on the basis of "hard data"—number and, hopefully, quality of publications, success in the grant-seeking mill, social success, offers from other universities which typically make their judgments on the basis of the same "hard data." And in this entire process, the qualities of the faculty member as teacher—his ability to convey ideas clearly, to incite interest and enthusiasm, to exemplify intellectual and moral integrity—these factors normally enter into the calculations of those who make decisions about salary and promotion, when they come in at all, on the basis of hunch, haphazard anecdote, and vague rumor.

Finally, students simply have a presumptive right to determine rules of student conduct. It has often been said that our society makes a fetish of youth. If so, society's indulgence has not been based on recognition of a person's developing capacity to take charge of his own destiny. The institutions of the university are often shot through with the spirit of paternalism. It is worse than absurd that youngsters old enough to embark on a college career, old enough to fight and die for their country, should be presumed so immature that they are not accorded the right to govern themselves in all nonacademic matters.

Functionally, acting *in loco parentis* is, in any event, primarily a means of putting students down, not protecting them. Though perhaps not the explicit intent of those who favor paternalism, there is here an attempt to keep tight rein on youths who the compact majority think are insufficiently tamed by careerism, and who are hence likely to swing between subversion and obscenity. That is to say, even the sincere claim that paternalistic institutions are justified because parents demand them or because it does students good to be subjected to them, is almost always ideologically self-deceptive. The myth that university students are children serves a larger political function. It constrains those various types of potential "troublemakers" who threaten the interests or sense of propriety of solid citizens who are never happier than when they are bending the wills of others to their own unreflective prejudices.

Administrators, pressed by students who demand a larger role in shaping university policies that affect their lives, often bleat about "beatniks," "Vietniks," "student syndicalists," and other forms of lower university life. Some of these administrators have even been known to incite public wrath by suggesting that sitting in some dark corner are sinister bearded characters who indefatigably plot new ways to make life miserable for everyone—especially university officials. Though not as sinister as these administrators seem to think, the bearded ones are undoubtedly there, sitting and scheming. And until universities meet their fundamental educational responsibilities to students, this is just as it should be.

8 AMERICAN
LIBERALISM
AND
FOREIGN
POLICY

Liberals are divided about United States Vietnam policy for
a number of reasons. They disagree about the policies that
best serve America's vital interests. They are at odds about
the morality of our intervention. They disagree about the
nature and threat of Communism and on the efficacy of military intervention as an instrument of American policy.

These differences are not new. They were more modestly
expressed during earlier crises—the Korean War, the intervention in Lebanon, the Bay of Pigs adventure, and even the
Cuban missile crisis. In the cases of Lebanon and the Bay
of Pigs, the issue was whether we had any business at all
being there. In the cases of Korea and the missile crisis,
liberal disagreement centered on the extent and nature of our
intervention.

Though disagreement on what best serves America's national interests appears to be straightforwardly factual, it is certain that judgments made on the basis of the inadequate evidence available to both supporters and critics of Administration policy are deeply affected by "internal prejudices." And moral beliefs are among the most powerful of the "prejudices" that shape such judgments. For example, it is clear that in matters affecting our relations with other nations the bugle call of old-fashioned patriotism is heard much more insistently by Vice President Humphrey than by Senator Fulbright. In domestic policy, Humphrey is no doubt a better liberal than Fulbright. But when confronted by the conflicting claims of a narrow patriotism and liberal morality, Humphrey, more consistently than Fulbright, has tended to dismiss the latter in favor of the former. This conflict between patriotism and morality poses the deepest and most perplexing problems for liberals trying to make judgments about foreign policy.

Liberal Morality and Patriotism

Most liberals have escaped the full force of the dilemma by being unduly optimistic about the inherent harmony between patriotic and liberal aims. In quiet moments they may question whether America's vital interests are invariably fused with the defense of freedom and democracy around the globe; but in the hurly-burly of public debate, they have not, until recently, found it difficult to convince themselves that America's authentic voice is the voice of Right. Their optimism has been reinforced by the development of nuclear military potential. For the existence of these terrible weapons makes it relatively easy to identify national interest with the peace of the world, and then to suppose that the deployment of national military power is required to preserve that peace. To suppose otherwise encourages appeasement on the model of Munich, and thereby increases the probability of nuclear showdown. Or so the familiar rationale goes.

The self-deception is aided by another factor. Because nations live in a "state of nature," the tendency to dismiss morality as irrelevant to policy seems to be strongest in the case of foreign policy. "We must not suppose," the amoralist assures us, "that in the absence of supranational law the claims of individual morality have application." Those who fear collectivism should be made to recognize that the real danger lies in this sort of collectivist abandonment of the strictures of individual morality. In no other area of public life can one have less confidence that professed moral commitments will be honored. Those schooled in the traditions of American Puritanism abandon their morality with remarkable ease when they turn their attention to foreign policy. Of course, they suffer the pangs of conscience for their sins. But the psychic pain is a small price to pay for the opportunity to prove to the powerful that good guys can be tough guys. Besides, remorse proves a most excellent expiation—a way of readying the spirit for the next sin.

Patriotic passions play a more influential role in foreign than domestic policy because national security seems more obviously involved. President Kennedy used to claim, "Domestic policy can only defeat us; foreign policy can kill us." This is true only for the short run. But with so much thought to be at stake it is not hard to understand why the relevance of more general moral concerns seems small.

The mischief encouraged by the view Kennedy held is then compounded by withholding or distorting information vital to rational assessment of foreign policy. The excuse invariably given is that the truth would jeopardize national security. Of course, more often than not, the truth would also embarrass officials.

There is another group of liberals who are very ready to

admit that patriotism may conflict with morality—and absolutely repudiate the former. They fancy that in so doing they are being good citizens and striking a blow against chauvinism. But the matter is not so simple. As a liberal, one may reject the claims of patriotism. As an American, he should not; nor, usually, can he. For as Americans we all have special obligations that we owe to other members of the national community. Only a person who *authentically* repudiates the system, and all the benefits it affords, can legitimately claim exemption from these special obligations. Socrates may have exaggerated these obligations when he sipped the hemlock; but he had a point.

The situation is similar to that faced by one who is both a liberal and a parent. As a liberal he is concerned equally about the welfare of every child. But as a parent, he both will and should consider the welfare of his own child in a special way. It is human and it is right to do so. Forced to choose between alternatives that might really harm his child and might really violate his political convictions, the parent has a definite obligation to give special, though not necessarily overriding, weight to his child's interests. Similarly, as a member of a national community—even one that falls far short of meeting the criteria of John Dewey's Great Community—if an individual more or less "consents" to the existing structure of social institutions, if he accepts its benefits, then he ought to acknowledge that he has some special obligations. (It must be dim acknowledgment of this point that partly accounts for the fact that many adopt the rhetoric, but not the reality, of revolutionary repudiation of American institutions.)

The visceral patriotism that is inculcated from birth is likely to find expression in any event. Too often it is expressed in an inverted form—through acts of dramatic protest that are more of a cry for a beloved country than an outcry against a hated system. It is simply better and more effective to avoid self-delusion, and to come to terms with one's own loyalties. That way one is not so tempted to deal with the hard and complex options of the moral life thoughtlessly—to exaggerate a nation's virtues, or its vices.

Yet reason also requires that the liberal should try to articulate the principles that ought to guide his judgment and action when forced to choose between his liberal commitments and his nation's narrower interests. Simple formulas are not available, but some things can be said.

First, the concern must be for *national* interests—interests that affect every American roughly equally. Too often the expressed concern for our "vital national interests" is nothing but a disguised effort to preserve or enhance one's power and privileges. Liberals should relentlessly expose those who invest the national interest with their own vested interests. Whether or not there is a single power elite, there are surely powerful elites that seek to make of American foreign policy an instrument of corporate aggrandizement. For example, there is little doubt that this country's unwillingness to do more than it does to bring down the viciously racist South African regime is in some part due to the fact that American investors are making profits at the rate of 25 per cent per year on their original investments in that brutal land.

Second, we should frankly recognize that there may be times when interests are vital without being national; or, worse, times when the nation has embarked on a fateful course without adequate justification. Under these conditions why should we expect or demand that everyone share equally in the sacrifices entailed? Let those who participate most in the potential benefits of the enterprise pay the heaviest price. Or let those who favor the enterprise strongly make the necessary sacrifices. At the very least, let us allocate this sacrifice randomly. It is a vicious patriotism that compels those who participate least in American freedom and affluence to share equally in its defense. It is more vicious when the sacrifice imposed is great—perhaps one's very life. It is yet more vicious when the sacrifice of those who benefit least is greater by far than that imposed on those who benefit most. To permit these things to happen is to make a mockery of the voluntarism that is supposed to be the operative principle of our free society.

The point does have practical application. A military system that penalizes the poor, the Negro, and the under-educated for the sin of being born without equal opportunity is a moral outrage. For another example, every time a planned expansion of desirable welfare programs is postponed in order to pay for military adventure, the rights of those in need are violated. (Here again our liberal leaders should acknowledge that failure to expand freedoms through acts of omission is no less a form of tyranny than elimination of freedoms that already exist. Rights can be denied as well as destroyed.)

Third, to the extent that the interests involved are national in the relevant sense, there should be a rough correlation between the importance of these interests and the human cost protecting them requires. It is principally this point that accounts for liberal dissent and division about Vietnam. What the American government has authorized for the sake of dubious interests and commitments is felt by many to be barbaric. Among these people are many who will even concede that American interests are indeed jeopardized. But they maintain that these interests are at best marginal—not remotely important enough to justify the heinousness of our means. The napalming and saturation bombing, the well-documented brain-washing and torture in which we have participated, the reckless misuse of our young combatants to prop a military regime that clearly lacks the support even of the part of the population within the regions still securely held—what is all of this but the moral counterpart of what Stalin and his cohorts did in Russia for the sake of industrial growth? The Stalinist nature of our means cannot begin to be justified by the marginal national interests allegedly being protected by a military policy that is not restrained enough.

Those of us who view matters in this way are simply less inclined than liberals like Vice President Humphrey to permit patriotism to override morality in the making of foreign policy.

We believe that liberal Administrations have too often tended to purchase immunity from the charge of being radical or socialistic in domestic policy by being especially tough and "amoral" in foreign policy. We know that many who are capable of thinking with fine-grained discrimination about our domestic problems often think in crudely stereotypic terms about the nature, interests, and moral claims of people in other lands. Liberals are not the worst offenders—but they are far from being immune to this disease of the moral imagination. There is nothing unusual nor particularly blameworthy about the tendency. With the best will in the world, liberal policy normally requires a subtlety of empirical discrimination that it is virtually impossible to achieve. For such distinctions must normally be drawn against a background of inadequate information and the cultural insensitivity that is bound to affect one born and bred in a very different culture. Americans who go abroad quickly recognize these defects in others. Why should they find it so difficult to understand that the very same cultural insularity is even more likely to characterize Americans themselves? For American culture has had to be even more constraining than most, if only because it has had to shape national character out of incredibly heterogeneous human beings. The type of American officials depicted in the novel *The Ugly American* are not just a national calamity, they are a human inevitability. "You Americans don't understand. You are making beggars of our children, prostitutes of our women, and Communists of our men!"—this was the rebuke hurled at a young American soldier by a South Vietnamese teacher when the soldier threw candy on the ground before a swarm of pleading children. The young American was only trying to be friendly.

The general thrust of the foregoing analysis is that, though

American liberals cannot be expected to subordinate national interests to the claims of morality on every occasion, they must make sure that these claims are not casually overridden on any occasion. The point, though abstract and difficult to apply concretely, is absolutely central. The main function of liberalism in the conduct of foreign policy is steadily and intelligently to maintain the relevance of liberal morality; to insure that neither ends nor means are fastened on the nation without relentless scrutiny from liberalism's moral point of view; to affirm that, in the balancing of narrower against wider interests, the latter are normally pre-eminent. I have tried to indicate how this perspective might be applied to the present Vietnam policy. Taken seriously, these abstract considerations would, for some, mean the difference between support and opposition to United States policy—a significant difference.

Moralism and Morality

There are those who regard any stress on the morality of foreign policy as defective—mere "moralism." Now it is true that great evil has often resulted from appeal to moral principles in the making of American foreign policy. This is so in part because problems of morality often have a surface simplicity that belies the underlying complexity of the factual and moral considerations involved. Thus many refuse the same sustained effort of intelligence in moral matters that they urge as a matter of course in areas of their technical competence. There are many brilliant technicians in our scientific culture who take a holiday from reason when they address themselves to moral problems—especially whenever questions of priority involving essentially vague concepts such as "national interest," "justice," "welfare," and "human rights" are at issue. But if, in making morality relevant to foreign policy, one tends to be less rigorously empirical, or to use pious moral rhetoric vacuously, or to think in terms of moral absolutes when the available alternatives are different shades of gray, or arrogantly to suppose that the specific institutions of one's native land provide the best models for every other society, or to suppose that there are no historical prerequisites for progressive change, the fault lies not in the effort to make morality relevant but in the thoughtlessness with which the effort is made. The remedy lies not in abandoning morality, but in embracing rationality. The mark of a truly advanced society is not only or mainly its superior technology, but also the quality of thought and morals that shape decisions of how to deploy the power its technology makes available.

Those in charge of the conduct of American foreign policy are often moralistic. They are too often implacably self-righteous, devoid of compassion. Their self-righteousness and lack of compassion have an epistemological consequence.

For to view the ferment in the underdeveloped nations of the world from the lofty height of a judging deity effectively screens out the agony that is the daily lot of millions of individual human beings. It incapacitates a person for the task of understanding revolutionary ferment. Arthur Schlesinger, Jr., analyzing Dean Rusk's participation in the Kennedy Administration, commented:

> At times one wondered whether the harshness of life—the seething planet of revolutionary violence, ferocity and hate, shadowed by nuclear holocaust—ever penetrated the screen of clichés, ever shook that imperturbable blandness.*

But Schlesinger errs in supposing that the moral insensitivity of men like Rusk is a personal fault; an accident of temperament. Rather the trait is a chronic disorder resulting from a social milieu that encourages us to view human beings as

* A *Thousand Days*, Boston, Houghton Mifflin, 1965, p. 434.

mere things, instruments of policy in the gigantic clash between the forces of light and the forces of darkness. Beneath
the "imperturbable blandness" of men like Rusk is a controlling passion for abstract freedom and abstract democracy
as ferocious in its consequences as the inquisitorial commitment to the Christian brotherhood of man and sovereignty
of the one true God.

It is at this point that theorists who view the application
of moral principles to the making of foreign policy come
back with what they regard as a clinching argument. "Whenever power is used," they say, "certain men use other men as
means. This is inherent in the very exercise of power. In the
conduct of foreign policy, power must be used; sin cannot,
therefore, be avoided." The argument is simple-minded. The
authority to whom appeal is usually made by such "realists"
is Kant. But Kant claimed something different. He wrote
that rational beings should treat all others as ends, "never
merely as means." (Kant's emphasis.) It is simply a non
sequitur to claim that this dictum implies that men are never
to be treated as means to some end. All it proscribes is that
this never be the whole of the treatment they are accorded.
What Kant's authority suggests, the common sense of
morality confirms. Those who exercise power do not inevitably sin. Whether the use of a person as a means is or is not
immoral depends on two factors: Are his claims as a human
being as fully respected as they should be? Are the ends pursued morally worthy? No doubt, it is not easy to decide in
particular situations. But if rape is likely, try to avoid it instead of moaning about man's depravity.

It is precisely because American statesmen like Rusk lack
compassion that they so often make mere means of individuals
our foreign policies affect. A liberal foreign policy would aim
at a world in which each person possesses the resources of

* In Chapter 2 of The Fundamental Principles of the Metaphysics
of Morals, London: Longmans, Green, 1909, p. 52.

materials, mind and spirit, as well as the opportunities, to carve out a career in conformity to that person's own nature and reasoned choice. At the same time, the policies directed to this end would not treat as mere means those who are meant to be the beneficiaries of our benevolence. Unfortunately, that is precisely how countless millions throughout the world are today regarded and dealt with by our policymakers. Vietnam provides only the most depressing example.

The Liberal Dialectic

Up to this point, I have dwelled on the relevance of liberal morality to foreign policy. But beyond morality lies a body of doctrines that are peculiarly relevant to this world of revolutionary tumult. For since liberals began to doubt that a free market economy was the answer to all liberal dreams, there has emerged a loose set of principles that help them to understand patterns of dynamic change; a sort of *liberal dialectic.*

It starts with the assumption that revolutions will be made by people who have come to believe that the abysmal poverty and arbitrary control of their lives are unnecessary. Once the feudal conviction that life must move in predestined grooves is shattered, revolution becomes inevitable unless those who rule buy off discontent with genuine social reform. Those who, in their misery, are busy making a revolution will have little time or inclination to worry as much as they perhaps should about the principles and values rightly cherished by relatively affluent liberals in relatively sophisticated societies. They want bread and relief from personal insecurity—in that order. There will be time enough, or so they think, to worry about freedom and democracy, in their more developed aspects, after the revolution. One does not have to approve of or refrain from criticizing the fact that revolutions are not humane. One simply recognizes that that is the way things are likely to happen; and that criticism without self-righteous blame is possible and desirable.

New forms of tyranny do inevitably result during the postrevolutionary period; but with a difference, if the tyranny is reimposed along with bread and the growth of modern industry. It is not necessary to be a Maoist to recognize that freedom and democracy will mean little to a populace that remembers too well the misery of life that has gone before. Nor is it necessary to suppose that the nature or extent of the tyranny that results is the same in different circumstances. India is far from being a liberal democracy; but the forms of oppression that exist there are far preferable to those that exist in China.

In any event, memories die, and tyranny produces new discontents, new forms of personal insecurity. Thus there is a re-emergence of the demand for institutions that foster relief from oppression and, eventually, the conditions of self-respect and the fuller development of human powers. The prerequisites and consequences of a growing industrial order —education and economic sufficiency—will insure that. Economic adequacy will provide the material base; education, the skills of mind and the qualities of spirit that encourage growth of the desire to achieve a progressively fuller control over one's own destiny. This will happen first in professional groups that the very imperatives of industrial growth absolutely require. The scientific and technological communities will hold an oppressive regime to ransom—and the ransom they will demand will be not only money, but relief from arbitrary exercise of power. That is, rule of law and personal autonomy will be established; at first in limited spheres and only precariously. But over time there will be an escalating demand for freedom, and the seeds of discontent will be sown in the society generally. For the exercise of freedom breeds new demands for freedom. Only ruthless oppression can block these developments; and such ruthlessness would prove industrially self-defeating.

Liberal progress may, therefore, receive many setbacks. But the human pressures generated will be relentless over time. The precipitating mechanism at every point will be what I earlier called the dialectic of disorder. For at each stage the rhetoric of change will outpace the change that is actually permitted. Those who are responsible for perpetrating the rhetorical fraud will find that they have truly sown the seeds, if not of their own violent destruction, at least of their peaceful demise.

History is on the side of liberalism—always supposing that history is not abruptly terminated by nuclear holocaust. This is so precisely because it is men who make history—men with their capacity for deceit, cupidity, irrationality, aggressiveness, bigotry; but also with their unquenchable desire for dignity and the fullest development of their human powers. If the dialectic gives liberals no advantage over Marxists in their ability to forecast the onset and course of revolutionary action, it does enable liberals more accurately to forecast the aftermath of revolutionary disorder.

After the Second World War, many liberals were fixated on the awesome tyranny of Stalin's regime. The "savage anti-Semitism, the turning over to the Gestapo of anti-Nazi refugees, the butchery of entire populations, the starvation of the peasantry and exploitation of the proletariat, the terrorizing of the intelligentsia and the exile to slave camps of uncounted millions,"[*] are enough to explain the fixation. Still, it remains a tragedy that, during the postwar period, many American liberals were so thrown into panic by Stalinist excesses that they failed to invoke the very principles of change that would have promoted a more flexible and, from the liberal point of view, more effective reaction to Stalinist

[*] H. Swados, "What's Left of the Left," *The Nation*, 100th Anniversary Issue, p. 113.

tyranny. A liberal as sensitive as George F. Kennan declared just before Stalin's death that the monolithic character of Stalinist Russia was not likely to be altered by peaceful, internal change. It can be truly claimed that most liberals had simply lost not only their heads but also touch with the insights of their own tradition. For Stalin's ruthless suppression of freedom was bound to produce precisely those forms of arbitrary government and, consequently, insecurity, indignity, and also the erosion of the self-respect that generates not only the demand for rule of law and constitutional order but also the yearning for freedom—not just on the lowest rungs of the social system, but on the highest as well. For no man rests easy when he might hear the midnight knock at his door. Thus, as the generations die who made the revolution and remember hunger too well, the spring of liberal aspiration—the desire freely to create one's own destiny—reasserts itself. It is happening in Russia; and it will happen in China.

Many will undoubtedly regard the foregoing as wildly optimistic. The deep cultural differences that so divide the peoples of the world—the rise of Nazism in one of the world's most industrialized and cultivated nations, the conflict within China, and the magnitude of the problems of population and economic disparities—will seem antithetical to the proposition that history belongs to liberalism.

The weight of historical evidence and the results of more systematic social inquiry do, however, seem to confirm the claim that human beings are not so very different; that the shaping influence of different cultures is undermined by the common institutions of industrial society. In every more advanced nation, cultural sophisticates fear the encroaching pressure of the "American way of life"—that is, of industrial civilization in its brassiest, most wasteful forms—more than any other social development. Nazi Germany was a political order destined either to conquer or to be destroyed. It was destroyed. Had it conquered, I believe the processes of the liberal dialectic would have occurred over a long stretch of time. Finally, the immense economic and population problems that exist are cause for alarm, but not for despair. For they can be dealt with, if only men have the will; we do not lack the necessary knowledge or the resources.

If only men have the will—that is crucial. The evidence for these optimistic assumptions is admittedly indeterminate. Yet, to repeat a point central to what has gone before, if the dialectic is a good conjecture, and if it is a possible outcome, then why should we not accept it as a basis for policy in order better to increase the probability of achieving a liberal society. Under conditions of indeterminacy, the pessimistic hypothesis is not less an ideological response, nor more empirical, than the optimistic hypothesis.

Moreover, the imperatives of social change in industrial society that have been articulated are premised on a judiciously optimistic conception of human nature. I am not denying man's flaws; only affirming that despite everything, there is also in him an unquenchable desire to carve out a career that is in conformity to his own nature and reasoned choice—in brief, to live the kind of life the liberal prescribes. Orwell's 1984 nightmare is an instructive projection of tendencies present in any society; but no more than that. For no society has moved very far down the road Orwell envisioned, without encountering barriers, and sometimes disaster. The desire for dignity rooted in self-esteem and the full development of one's own powers seems in time to be renewed, no matter how individuals are oppressed.

Communism and Revolution

What emerges from these arguments are two points of transcendent importance for present American foreign policy.

First, Communist societies are not more heinous nor resistant to pressures making for progressive internal change than many other tyrannies that have plagued men in history. Indeed, in some ways they are more susceptible to such change—because the scientific, technological, and educational growth they inevitably foster do create those seeds of discontent that set the liberal dialectic into motion. Yugoslavia provides the best support for this optimistic assessment. Today, only two decades after the Yugoslav Communist party assumed power, it is in the process of abdicating from exclusive executive power and is instead adopting the role of guide and stimulus to the nation.* Whether this change is more formal than real remains to be seen. But few objective observers of what has been happening in Yugoslavia would deny that, though organized opposition to the Communist party has not to this point in time been permitted, the participatory institutions that exist in industry and increasingly in politics have acquired considerably more than merely formal authority. If the account of the nature and threat of Communism here proposed were to gain general acceptance in the United States, the still far too rigid lines of American cold-war policy would be profoundly modified.

Second, America's almost invariable response to revolutionary disorder—the rhetoric of the carrot, the substance of the stick—has proved a failure. At the present time military power is viewed as the main instrument of American policy, economic, political, cultural, and educational assistance as ancillary. Unless this order of priorities is reversed, there can be no escape from a pattern that has led to a mounting succession of disasters in foreign policy.

---

* In a comment on these developments, Edward Crankshaw writes: "The proposed dismantling of the Yugoslav Communist party apparatus, the surrender of the levers of power by an entrenched ruling class of privileged functionaries, is an undertaking of positively stunning sweep and boldness. Its implications for the Communist world in general are quite beyond the imagination at this stage, but are obviously complex and exciting to a degree. Marshal Tito for the second time in his career (the first was the defiance of Stalin in 1948) has started off a great process which will change the mood of history." The Observer (London), June 19, 1966.

To adopt this perspective is not to contend that we should dismantle our military shield: only that it be used to further, not, as presently tends to be the case, to defeat, liberal aims around the globe. As Walter Lippmann tentatively put it:

> . . . in the backward and undeveloped regions of the globe, military power and political influence are antithetical. In order to exercise influence, political, economic, cultural, technical, it is necessary to limit military intervention to those rare instances where there is a clear and present danger to an indubitable vital interest.*

At the moment, many liberals who in principle favor the proposed reversal of priorities are fearful of implementing the required programs of assistance because of the way they have been used to provide a rationale for American military adventure in Vietnam and elsewhere. But the solution to this problem is not to abandon such programs, but to administer them differently. Increasingly, our assistance should be put at the disposal of international agencies in whose independence both we and the recipient nations can have confidence. In this way the use of such aid as a pretext for military intervention can be prevented. In this way also the institutions of international order can be strengthened; the cause of world peace more effectively served.

China and Vietnam

There is a sophisticated response to these arguments—one that I am convinced lies at the heart of present American foreign policy. It is the claim that, though the optimistic assumptions implicit in the dialectical view may prove correct, there is also the possibility of ruin if we discount the bellicose rhetoric of our adversaries. Responsible officials may hope for the best, but it is their duty to plan for the worst.

* *Newsweek*, June 20, 1966.

For example, though China may be adolescent in her present expression of fear of our aggressive intent, she happens also to be in a position to jeopardize vital American interests before she grows up. Though she may not yet have matched her deeds to increasingly abrasive words, she may yet do so. Any American government that did not maintain sufficient military power, strategically deployed and, where necessary, actively engaged to forestall that contingency, would be irresponsible.

In the last analysis, this is the reason for our intervention in Vietnam; this is why we have ringed China with the most awesome military potential ever possessed by a nation; this is why we have so emphasized military might at the expense of economic effort throughout Asia. The public rationale that emphasizes our commitments and our benevolence is of negligible importance by comparison with this allegedly prudent desire to cope with genuine dangers to our vital national interests.

To accept the foregoing argument amounts to abandonment of the demand that liberal morality be made relevant to foreign policy. For it rests on the assumption that any means which effectively counter the *possible*—not *probable*—threat to vital national interests is permissible. And so, if statesmen are convinced that despicable means are effective, despicable means will be used. Human beings will be squandered in order to forestall possible outcomes. The remoteness and the massiveness of the evil make it banal, therefore tolerable.

I do not deny that great evils may be required to forestall even greater ones. But is it too much to ask that the adoption of inhuman means be a response, not to the mere possibility, but to the *probability* of national disaster?

And, in any event, the contingency argument cuts both ways. For it is also *possible* that our policies in Southeast Asia will precipitate nuclear war. Which contingency are we to plan for: the possibility of nuclear war precipitated by de-escalation or the possibility of nuclear war precipitated by escalation? Assuming good will, both aim at preserving the peace. The reasonable alternative cannot be decided without careful appeal to evidence. But the Administration's record of erroneous prediction in Southeast Asia provides little basis for confidence in its assumptions or its ability to assess evidence objectively.

Consider the following record. On February 25, 1963, Senator Mansfield, after a fact-finding trip to Vietnam reported to President Kennedy:

> Those who bear responsibility for directing operations under the new strategy are optimistic over prospects for success. Indeed, success was predicted to the group [of senators] almost without exception, by responsible Americans and Vietnamese, in terms of a year or two hence.

In a footnote, Senator Mansfield added that Admiral Harry Felt more cautiously predicted that it might take three years. Three years later, almost to the day, President Johnson ordered the bombing of North Vietnam. Four years later, there were over 280,00 men in South Vietnam, and more than 500,000 are there now. In May, 1963, Secretary of Defense McNamara announced that we had turned the corner in Vietnam. On October 2, 1963, he and General Taylor reported to President Kennedy that in "their judgment the major part of the U.S. military task can be completed by the end of 1965." On February 18, 1964, Secretary McNamara predicted, in testimony before the Congress, that the "bulk" of U.S. forces could be expected to leave by 1965.

After the war's escalation in February 1965, the Administration justified its course in terms of the following considerations:

i. Air strikes would stem the flow of men and materials from North Vietnam into the South.

ii. The show of force would weaken our adversaries' will to fight.

iii. Air strikes would hearten our allies and dismay Peking.

iv. The air strikes would diminish the need to send large numbers of conventional forces.

v. Escalation would stabilize the political situation in the South.

Two and a half years later, not one of these predictions has been proved accurate. In fact, on January 20, 1966, in his report, this time to President Johnson, Senator Mansfield said:

> . . . the fact is that [the present South Vietnamese government is], as other Vietnamese governments have been over the past decade, at the beginning of a beginning in dealing with the problems of popular mobilization in support of the government.

Even the apparent stability of the South Vietnamese regime is sustained by American arms, not intrinsic political strength.

To the dismal record of wrong prediction must be added all the reasons for distrusting the judgments of public officials described in the section that dealt with the politics of pseudo-realism.

The Administration's fears of the Chinese threat to our national security and its assumptions about how best to cope with that threat have the semblance of reason. But when put to the test of available evidence, they are exposed for what they are—the approximate counterpart of the less reasonably expressed fears of the Communist Chinese about America's aggressive intent.

The Politics of Radical Pressure in the Making of Foreign Policy

What ought critics do? Many believe that nothing can be done **until** the structure of American society is transformed. They argue that reason and conventional political pressure cannot drive a wedge between those corporate groups that determine the shape of present policies and those directly responsible for making those policies. They accept C. Wright Mills' thesis that "In so far as national events are decided, the power elite are those who decide them."* And, like Mills, they regard decisions having to do with issues of war and peace as "national events."

At the same time, they tend to ignore other claims Mills made—albeit, incoherently. "Any contemporary re-statement of liberal and socialist goals," he wrote, "must include as central the idea of a society in which all men would become men of substantive reason, whose independent reasoning would have structural consequences for their society, its history, and thus for their own life fates."† And, developing the strategic implications of this view, he also claimed that though we live in a society that is democratic mainly in its legal forms and its formal expectations, "we ought not to minimize the enormous value and the considerable opportunity these circumstances make available."‡ That is, one tendency of Mills' thought leads straight to what I have called the politics of radical pressure. And such tactics *cannot effectively influence foreign policy* if there exists a power elite that is monolithic and impervious to the constraints of reason and peripheral pressure. In their frustration, those

* *The Power Elite,* New York, Oxford University Press, 1956, p. 18.
† *The Sociological Imagination,* New York, Oxford University Press, 1959, pp. 173-4.
‡ *Ibid.,* p. 191.

who believe that such an elite does exist tend to practice the politics of self-indulgence. But the consequences of this posture for the making of foreign policy are at best unhelpful, at worst a tactical boon to those who defend Administration policies.

Even if structural change is required to alter the central tendencies of American foreign policy in desired ways (and I am not sure that this is so), there are good reasons for qualified optimism about our ability to change these policies in important respects.

1. Capitalist systems are even more diverse and complex than Communist systems. Again and again Marxists and socialists have had to learn that the institutions of countries like the United States are resilient enough to defeat their ominous predictions. Not only does even formal democracy make a significant difference, not only are our precariously established civil liberties nevertheless real, not only do many of the policies adopted by powerful interests for their own selfish reasons have unanticipated but beneficial consequences; but the powerful groups that constitute our "power elite" often have different and competing interests. And this fact is often reflected in conflicting ideas about foreign policy.

Not just the poor or those concerned about civil rights, but also those concerned about urban development, education, health, old-age, and conservation must view with considerable misgiving the existing budgetary priorities. They would like to lay their hands on the sums being allocated for the Vietnam War—especially when they are doubtful that that war really is required for the protection of America's vital interests.

The strategic possibility that presently exists for altering the course of events is greater than most opponents of Administration policies realize. For increasingly even the hawks are implicitly acknowledging that the war does not serve our vital interests. Conservative hawks like Senators Richard

Russell and John Tower argued that we should either step up our commitment in order to finish the job quickly, or get out. But if they are serious about the latter, then they must believe that getting out would not jeopardize American security. And liberal hawks like G. Mennen Williams have argued that—though we should support the President's present policy of restrained militarism, because American security is at stake—if free elections bring to power a Vietnamese government that asks the United States to leave, we should exit quietly.

As he admits that we may be obligated to leave prior to having crushed the "aggression," he is implicitly conceding that our intervention may not be essential to American security after all. Otherwise, as a patriotic and responsible American, he could not seriously contemplate leaving the field to the Communists *under any conditions.* The incoherence of both groups of hawks makes them very vulnerable to attack within the framework of conventional politics. The opportunities for those prepared to practice the politics of radical pressure with skill and determination are great.

2. Even if a power elite exists, there is little reason to suppose that its members have identical interests or even perceive developments in precisely the same ways. Let us suppose, for the purposes of argument, that men like Johnson and Kennedy, Goldwater and Hatfield, Curtis Le May and James Gavin are all members of this power elite. Let us even admit that their theoretical differences are at best marginal. It remains true that those slight differences are translatable into policy differences that could have momentous consequences for human civilization. The difference between nuclear holocaust and even a succession of brush-fire wars is no small matter. It does, after all, make sense in such circumstances to support men and positions with whose general outlook we disagree. For them to ascend to power might mark the difference between total disaster and less fateful evil.

At the same time the politics of radical pressure require

that struggle should proceed on two levels. Not only must we make the best of the available and defective alternatives in the short run, but we must strive to insure that the options that exist in the long run are much wider than is presently the case. We must work to create a "new (liberal) politics," to elect a more sensible Administration in 1968, to bring pressure on the Nervous Nellies who speak in the accents of the doves but embrace the policies of the hawks, to strengthen the hand of the present Administration against the pressures of the super-hawks—and we must work for all these things simultaneously. For success in each case could mark a fateful difference. It is callously glib, even inhuman, to claim that between say, Senator Kennedy's views and President Johnson's, or between Johnson's and Goldwater's, there is nothing to choose. To take such positions is to abandon all effort to make intelligent discriminations—to abandon the traditions of reason.

3. Finally, as C. Wright Mills recognized when he was not completely bemused by his theory of the power elite, there are many who manage to have acquired reason and the capacity for morally autonomous judgment despite the faults of existing social conditions. That they retain these powers of mind and spirit despite the tremendous effort to undermine them made by men who, like President Johnson, identify responsible dissent with lack of masculinity is a tribute not only to the strength of the dissenters but also to a social system resilient enough to enable them to stand firmly against great power. The system that permits such things to happen possesses potentialities which, if more fully exploited, would increase the amount of opposition. When all the evils of the American social system have been counted, a moment should be spared to count its virtues.

There are thus degrees of political freedom that are not always acknowledged by those who prefer rather to denounce the system and make an occasional dramatic noise than to work persistently and carefully toward achievable policy goals. There are also certain tactics that more persistent individuals embrace, tactics that ought to be repudiated because they are self-indulgently self-defeating.

It is not inconsistent for someone to stress the likelihood of progressive change within diverse Communist societies, and yet for tactical and moral reasons to refuse to associate with domestic Communists in certain ways. As Irving Howe recently put it, the Communists have a right to their own house, but not a right to exist in mine (nor, for that matter, as tightly disciplined Communist parties have long made clear, for me to exist in theirs). Those who deny that their moral commitments are relevant to the forms of voluntary association they embrace or who weaken their tactical position by self-righteously proclaiming that exclusion of Communists (or, for that matter, antivivisectionists) is in principle repugnant, have in effect succumbed to a form of inverted McCarthyism. Without intending to, or even being aware of it, they permit their thought and action to be contaminated by the mindless anti-Communism it is their aim to combat. It is, after all, possible to possess both courage and moral integrity without embracing foolish tactics.

Similarly, whether one likes it or not, patriotism is a force with which those who hope to effect desirable political aims must reckon. To flaunt this sentiment by forms of protest that do little more than confirm one's own masculinity is the counterpart of that which makes the tough guys in government reject counsels of reason and morality.

Moreover, as I argued earlier, some patriotic concerns are legitimate. Unless one is prepared to match revolutionary deed to revolutionary rhetoric, Americans have an obligation to give weight to national prestige and other short-range national interests. Give weight—no more. Only one who willfully wishes to distort this point will insist that its admission capitulates to powerful political forces it has been the main business of this essay to criticize.

Finally, as I indicated earlier, the tactics and strategies that have proved so successful in the struggle for civil rights do not, in general, provide an appropriate model for the politics of foreign policy. Too often, however, the important dissimilarities have been ignored; the tactics of the civil rights movement, casually, and fruitlessly, applied to the fight for a better foreign policy. Perhaps the most important difference is the vital role civil rights direct-action techniques have played in dispelling the fear of those oppressed, the apathy of the convinced. But the problem in foreign policy is primarily that of convincing the unconvinced. Moral argument and appeal to self-interest are the most effective means of achieving these aims. The more dramatic forms of protest are likely to prove self-defeating. On the other hand, I do not want to deny that the tactics of the civil rights movement may be useful, especially when, as in the case of the teach-ins, they are creatively modified. I want to insist only that their use ought to be based on careful tactical calculations.

Liberals are opposing Administration policies in increasing numbers. This is so despite their instinctive aversion both to repudiating the policies of a liberal Administration and the form some opposition has taken. But their change of heart will prove futile unless they steer a coldly reflective course between self-indulgence and pseudo-realism. The fate of their nation, of mankind itself, may depend on the resoluteness with which they affirm their independent commitments and the effectiveness with which they practice the politics of radical pressure.

BIBLIOGRAPHY

Books

Education at Berkeley. Academic Senate of the University of California in Berkeley, Report of the Select Committee on Education. Berkeley, California: University of California Press, 1966.

Cobb, Charlie, et al. Thoughts of Young Radicals. New Jersey: The New Republic Books, 1966.

Connolly, William E. Political Science and Ideology. New York: Atherton Press, 1967.

Dewey, John. The Public and Its Problems (3rd edition). Denver: Alan Swallow, 1957.

DuBois, W. E. B. The Souls of Black Folk. Greenwich, Connecticut: Fawcett Publications, 1964.

Fanon, Frantz. The Wretched of the Earth. New York: Grove Press, 1966.

Freedom Budget for All Americans. New York: A. Philip Randolph Institute, 1966.

Fulbright, J. W. The Arrogance of Power. New York: Vintage Books, 1967.

Gardner, John. Excellence. New York: Harper & Row, 1961.

Hobbes, Thomas. The Leviathan: Parts I and II. New York: The Liberal Arts Press, 1958.

Hobhouse, Leonard T. *Liberalism*. New York: Oxford University Press, 1964.

Howe, Irving (ed.) *The Radical Papers*. New York: Doubleday, 1966.

James, William. *Pragmatism*. New York: Longmans, Green, 1946.

————. *Essays in Pragmatism*. New York: Hafner Publishing, 1954.

Kant, Immanuel. *Fundamental Principles of the Metaphysics of Morals*. New York and London: Longmans, Green, 1909.

Kerr, Clark. *The Uses of the University*. Cambridge: Harvard University Press, 1963.

Madison, James. "Federalist Paper Number Ten," *The Federalist*, ed. E. M. Earle. New York: The Modern Library, 1937.

Malcolm X. *The Autobiography of Malcolm X*. New York: Grove Press, 1966.

Marx, Karl. *Early Writings*. Translated and edited by T. B. Bottomore. New York: McGraw-Hill, 1963.

Michels, Robert. *Political Parties*. New York: The Free Press, 1949.

Mill, John Stuart. *Representative Government*. New York: The Liberal Arts Press, 1958.

Mills, C. Wright. *The Power Elite*. New York: Oxford University Press, 1959.

————. *The Sociological Imagination*. New York: Oxford University Press, 1959.

Myrdal, Gunnar. *Beyond the Welfare State*. New Haven: Yale University Press, 1960.

Niebuhr, Reinhold. *Moral Man and Immoral Society*. New York: Scribner's, 1952.

Petrovic, Gajo. *Marx in the Mid-Twentieth Century*. New York: Doubleday, 1967.

Rousseau, Jean Jacques. *The Social Contract*. New York: Hafner Publishing, 1947.

Schlesinger, Arthur, Jr. *A Thousand Days*. Boston: Houghton Mifflin, 1965.

Schumpeter, Joseph. *Capitalism, Socialism and Democracy* (3rd edition). New York: Harper & Row, 1950.

Thoreau, Henry David. *Walden and Other Writings*, ed. Joseph Wood Krutch. New York: Bantam Books, 1962.

Veblen, Thorstein. *The Theory of the Leisure Class*. New York: The New American Library, 1953.

Articles

Aiken, Henry D. "The American University: Part 1," *The New York Review of Books*, November 3, 1966.

————. "The University: Part II, What Is a Liberal Education?" *The New York Review of Books*, November 3, 1966.

Carmichael, Stokely. "What We Want," *The New York Review of Books*, September 22, 1966.

Danzig, David. "The Defense of Black Power," *Commentary*, September 1966.

Ferry, W. H. "The Brutalization of Violence," *Liberation*, October 1965.

Good, Paul. "A Tale of Two Cities," *The Nation*, November 21, 1966.

Gross, Ronald, and Judith Murphy. "New York's Late-Blooming University," *Harpers Magazine*, December 1966.

Howe, Irving. "New Styles in Leftism," *Dissent*, Summer 1965.

Kaufman, Arnold. "Murder in Tuskegee: Day of Wrath in the Model Town," *The Nation*, January 31, 1966.

————. "Radicalism and Conventional Politics," *Dissent*, July–August 1967.

Kopkind, Andrew. "The Future of Black Power," *The New Republic*, January 7, 1967.

Lin Piao. "Excerpts from Peking Declaration Urging 'People's War' to Destroy U.S.," *The New York Times*, September 4, 1965.

Rustin, Bayard. "Black Power and Coalition Politics," *Commentary*, September 1966.

Swados, Harvey, "The UAW and Walter Reuther," *Dissent*, Autumn 1963.

————. "What's Left of the Left," *The Nation* 100th Anniversary Issue, 1965.

Weiss, John. "The University as Corporation," *New University Thought*, Summer 1965.

INDEX

ABOUT THE AUTHOR

Arnold S. Kaufman, Professor of Philosophy at UCLA, was awarded his doctorate by Columbia University. He received his earlier education in Connecticut and New York City and studied for two years on a Fulbright Scholarship at the London School of Economics and at Oxford University. Since then he has returned to England for a year of research and lecturing. More recently he has been a Fellow at the Center for Advanced Study in the Behavioral Sciences at Stanford and a visiting professor of philosophy at Tuskegee, Harvard, and UCLA, has lectured at many other colleges and universities, including Reed, Stanford, and the universities of Washington, Colorado, and California at Berkeley, and in Yugoslavia at the universities of Belgrade and Sarajevo.

Involvement in the social problems of today has led Professor Kaufman into many other areas of social and intellectual concern. Long active in the civil rights movement, he worked in CORE and the NAACP for many years. He was one of the founders of the teach-in movement; and was one of the principal organizers of the National Teach-in held in Washington, D.C., in May 1965. He was one of the original organizers of the Dump-Johnson movement, and worked in the primary campaigns of 1968. A member of the Steering Committee of the Coalition for an Open Convention, he helped organize the New Democratic Coalition and is a member of its temporary National Steering Committee. He is also a member of the National Board of SANE and is active in the Vietnam Moratorium.